YOUTH TO THE RESCUE

YOUTH TO THE RESCUE

An Important Study of Youth's Response
to
The Challenge of Human Problems

by

LAWRENCE C. BAILEY

Published by
ARTHUR JAMES LIMITED
THE DRIFT, EVESHAM, WORCS.

First Edition 1967

© Lawrence C. Bailey—1967

All rights reserved by the Publishers,
Arthur James Limited of Evesham, Worcs., England

SBN : 85305 000 7

MADE AND PRINTED IN GREAT BRITAIN BY PURNELL AND SONS, LTD.
PAULTON (SOMERSET) AND LONDON

DEDICATED TO ALL YOUNG VOLUNTEERS
WHO BY THEIR ENERGY AND DEVOTION ARE CHANGING
THE SOCIAL PATTERN OF BRITAIN TODAY
AND IN PARTICULAR
TO MY YOUNG FRIENDS OF SOLIHULL AND BIRMINGHAM
WITH WHOM IT HAS BEEN MY PRIVILEGE
TO WORK

ACKNOWLEDGMENTS

The author is grateful to the *Birmingham Post and Mail* and to his colleague, Mary Hopson, for permission to reproduce the photographs in this book.

PREFACE

by Sir Edward C. G. Boyle, P.C., M.P.
Former Minister of Education

THE CHAIRMAN of the Birmingham Young Volunteers Trust has written a most valuable book about voluntary service by young people which will, I hope, reach a wide audience. Mr. Bailey has drawn upon his wide knowledge of the work both of the B.Y.V.T. and of the Birmingham Association of Youth Clubs in meeting co-operatively the community needs of one of our largest cities, and also upon his personal experience as President of the Solihull Young Volunteers.

No one could be better qualified to write this book, and Mr. Bailey's experience is matched by the humanity and sanity of his approach. He is both an idealist and a realist, who understands that the ideal of service needs to be presented to young people in a context whose relevance they can themselves easily "conceive and understand." How often I have been reminded by experienced Principals and Lecturers in Colleges of Education that discussion of ethical values, if it is to strike home, must be related to real-life situations and objectives which students can (as Keats would have said) "feel upon the pulse."

Mr. Bailey is also surely right when he reminds us that Once young people begin to think that community service is something that the adult world is telling them to do, they will shy from it. Only when it is their own natural

response to need and challenge will they become whole
hearted." I have always believed in the importance of the
teacher's duty (and the same goes for the youth leader) not
to try to impose his own moral standards on young people
but rather to help them towards forming a sense of values
and of standards with which they can genuinely feel
identified.

Finally, I would endorse Mr. Bailey's warning against
relying too much on "initial waves of enthusiasm." As he
so rightly comments, "It is comparatively easy to arouse
emotional zeal among young people. The problem is to
sustain it in practical action over a period of years." Perhaps we may usefully recall that it was not a man of
"emotional zeal" but a cool eighteenth-century sceptic who,
in the last words he ever wrote, reached the admirable
conclusion that "Upon the whole it seems undeniable that
nothing can bestow more merit on any human creature
than the sentiment of benevolence in an eminent degree."
Mr. Bailey is a man of faith in a sense that David Hume,
the author of those words, was not; yet both are at one in
the high value they set on "benevolence"—that is to say,
generosity, a love of humanity, and a disposition "to do
good" and to lend a helping hand whenever and wherever
the opportunity presents itself.

EDWARD C. G. BOYLE

House of Commons,
London S.W.1.
1967.

FOREWORD

Mine, too, was a Warwickshire school—not so many miles from the setting of this book, Solihull. In chapel our eyes were drawn to a carved profile that seemed to personify the nobility of youthful sacrifice, whilst the lines beneath—*If I should die, think only this of me, That there's some corner of a foreign field That is for ever England*—reflected an idealism which we accepted as our own. A few of us might have been dimly aware that another Old Boy, William Temple, was striving to relate idealism to the social problems of those inter-war years, but it was Rupert Brooke's imagery that prevailed.

As we passed the back streets between Rugby Station and the School it seldom occurred to us that they might contain lives stunted by deprivation or loneliness—still less that it lay in our power, there and then, to do anything for them.

And now in some hundreds of schools throughout the country young people are tackling situations of need, making a contribution of practical compassion and in so doing finding a sense of personal fulfilment. Brian Phythian at the Manchester Grammar School, George Eustance at Calday Grange, Neil Paterson at Sevenoaks, and Lawrence Bailey at Solihull have been amongst the pioneers of this movement. Their impact extends far beyond the geographical surroundings of their schools. That young people in York, for example, should today be working amongst mental patients at Clifton Hospital is due to David Scott, whose contribution as a schoolboy is so tellingly described in the chapter "Breaking Down the Barriers." For David, on leaving Solihull, volunteered to be transplanted to Merchant Taylors' School at Northwood—and within weeks so succeeded in immersing boys there in work at local mental hospitals that some of them, in turn, offered themselves for similar service elsewhere in Britain. There can be chain-reactions in human generosity.

Britain has shown a capacity this century for producing every twenty years or so some fresh manifestation of adventurous training—Scouting, Outward Bound, the Duke of Edinburgh's Award, to mention only a few—from which tens of thousands of young people have immeasurably benefited. But adventurous training is not exactly synonymous with actual service. The implications of confronting the young with real-life situations of human need, with death even (which Lawrence Bailey faces in his chapter on "Hospitals and Homes") are more controversial, more difficult—and so much more significant. There was a moment just after 1945 when it seemed as though the Welfare State might result in voluntary service, if not becoming superfluous then concerning itself only with marginal tasks. Now we are entering an era where it is implicit in the nature of our social problems that we can no longer pay others to do our loving for us. We have to move beyond the structure of the Welfare State, dependent on a cadre of professional experts, towards the concept of a participant society, a compassionate community.

If young volunteers have a contribution to make in the jungles of Africa and Asia, they have surely something to give in the wildernesses of their own country. How slow we are to think, as a nation, of what young people might do in times of crisis, has been highlighted by Aberfan and the Torrey Canyon oil disaster: the insight that inspired

Baden-Powell to make imaginative use of young volunteers
at Mafeking is not conspicuous in high places today,
though something akin to siege conditions may be dis-
cerned in some of our social problems no less than in
physical emergencies. Yet the conviction that we need the
young, as much as they themselves want to be used, does
grow. It can be seen in the emergence of organisations such
as Young Volunteers of Merseyside, Sheffield's Youth
Action and Birmingham's Young Volunteers' Trust. St.
Thomas's Hospital, London, and the Fulbourne Mental
Hospital, Cambridge, have recently appointed full-time
organisers of voluntary service—and Probation Officers are
considering how most effective use may be made of volunteers in their field.

Not only Lawrence Bailey's able arguments but the facts
themselves also refute the sophisticated criticisms of this
movement as comprising adolescent Lady Bountifuls
undertaking middle-class do-goodery. More and more Chief
Constables are exposing cadets to situations of social stress
in the belief that awareness of human problems may be the
most vital part of their training; should industry do like-
wise with their young employees then the consequences
could be far-reaching. The Newsom Report, "Half Our
Future", specifically urged that Secondary Modern pupils
in their last year be enabled to have some experience of
community service. The implications of this development
could be profound. "I've no time for this 'Service' stuff,
just give me a job to do," remarked one such boy—and one
knows what he meant. The possibility may even exist that
helping others comes to be regarded as something only for
early-leavers and the under-endowed, whilst examination
pressures are held to excuse from social action the academ-
ically ambitious—an illegitimate élite.

Many lessons emerge from this book that are valid far beyond the world of Solihull, of school and even of social service: that financial provision is secondary to the reality and urgency of the demands made on volunteers: that preoccupation with motivation is irrelevant when there are human needs to be met: that the young handicapped yearn to be treated not as passive recipients of aid but as active participants in giving: that it is primarily adult attitudes that have to be changed, in showing a greater readiness to accept the service of the young. "If you set too good an example here, you're crucified," wrote a boy who had volunteered to share life in a Borstal.

The value of this book is that it shows what can be achieved, not by heroes reacting to exceptional challenges, but by ordinary young people concerned with the needs about them.

ALEC DICKSON
Founder of Voluntary Service Overseas and
Founder and Hon. Director of
Community Service Volunteers, London.

CONTENTS

Chapter 1

INTO ACTION

He surveyed the house dispassionately, almost numbly. It looked drab and bleak against the glittering background of snow. The steep roof hung heavy and white against the leaden sky. Broken window panes and dirty flaking paintwork seemed oddly out of place beside the even neatness of the world around. It was the last one in the terrace, and here alone winter's icy grip appeared to have taken a complete hold.

"It's an adult game, this community service lark," he thought, as he hammered on the scratched door for the third time, "a grown-up's device for keeping us occupied. Still, they said there was an old chap living here who might need some help."

He beat his arms against his thick duffle-coat to keep himself warm, and pulled the hood more closely round his nipped ears. It seemed a long wait. Then he observed that the door was slightly open. He considered for a moment. Back doors were not usually open unless someone was at home. So he gave it a gentle push. It creaked. He called in, but still there was no answer.

"Better take a look," he thought, "there must be someone about. The snow wants clearing from the path, anyway."

He went through the bare scullery, pausing nervously. The door leading into the back room was half open. He

peeped in at the dismal grey room. His eye rested fleetingly
on the half-peeled wallpaper, the dust-laden curtains and the
bare black grate, all in the half-light of a late winter afternoon. A sudden rustling sound made him start quickly, with
the surprised shock of realisation that he was not alone.

There, huddled in a low, black leather armchair, its
horsehair stuffing bulging uncouthly from the worn
patches, was a very old man. His face was as grey as the
colourless wallpaper, and his eyes, staring blankly into the
empty fireplace, seemed dull and uncomprehending.

"God," the boy thought, "how old he looks! How old,
and alone, and how perished!"

The old man coughed a rasping, chesty cough from deep
down. His frail body shook. The boy cleared his own throat
and introduced himself self-consciously.

"I've come to see if I can help," he said. "I'm a volunteer
you see—from the school over the way—don't want anything—just to help. Sorry to burst in, but you didn't hear
the knocking—so I thought——"

His stumbling apology tailed off as the old man turned,
more startled even than his young visitor had been. He
pressed his tired hands upon the arms of his chair, tried
vainly to rise and slumped back, pathetically.

"Get out!" he gasped, between coughs. "Get out! You've
broken enough of my windows as it is. What more do you
want? You young vandals are all the same."

The boy stood his ground hesitantly. "I'll make you a
cup of tea," he said.

This was his great stand-by in social service. Always offer
to make a cup of tea. If they don't want you to, they'll
make one for you just the same. Then you're in. Cups of
tea—that's what this business is all about—cups of tea with
old ladies—or old men—nothing to it!

But somehow his thoughts did not ring true this time. Instead he felt an odd lump in his throat that he had not felt before. Not that he was given to sentiment. He'd hate the person who dared suggest as much, but this old fellow and his awful set-up, well——

The old man wheezed his reply between spluttered eruptions. "There's no water—all frozen up—lavatory frozen—taps—the lot. Now be off with you! You've no right coming here to make fun of an old man."

His coughing grew worse. The boy turned to go, hesitated, and changed his mind. He crossed over to the old man and looked with the fresh confidence of youth into his anxious, lined face.

"Right then, I'm going, but I'll be back. I'll be back. You'll see."

With flushed eagerness he sped back to school over the snow-laden fields to his fellow volunteers and the master in charge of voluntary service.

"Sir," he blurted, unable to speak quickly enough, "there's an old man over there," pointing excitedly, wildly, across the fields, "who really needs us—he really does! He's all alone. His house is frozen up. He looks like death. I reckon he won't last the winter out if we don't help him. We've just got to do something!"

The rescue began at once. Cups of tea with old ladies suddenly became an irrelevant joke. Snow was cleared. A pit was dug in the frozen garden for refuse. Water was fetched and tea made. Someone went for the plumber. Pipes were unfrozen. Bags of coal appeared as if by magic. Wood was chopped in great quantity. Soon a warm fire blazed away, its friendly light flickering on the once gloomy walls. Volunteers abounded. No job was too large; no trouble too much.

The old man, a periodic sufferer from bronchial pneumonia, found miraculously the warmth, comfort and companionship he had not known for years.

Youth had come to the rescue!

This story, based on an early incident in the life of the Solihull School Voluntary Service Group, is true in all essentials. It breathed life into the Group in a way nothing else had done until that moment, early in 1963.

A few months earlier the Group had been created in response to a request from the Headmasters' Conference in 1962. Winchester, Marlborough and Solihull were asked to find ways of liberalising the activities of the Combined Cadet Forces. One of the ways in which Solihull responded to that request was to create for boys in the C.C.F. age range an alternative in the form of a Voluntary Service Group.

Before agreeing to undertake responsibility for such a group, I felt it important to insist that it should be entirely separate in organisation and control from the C.C.F., and based upon a genuine voluntary system. This was agreed, and no boys were accepted unless they offered to serve of their own free will. To discourage boys from volunteering from wrong motives, it was made clear that volunteers must be prepared to work longer hours than cadets on Corps afternoons. They must also give evening or weekend community service in their own time and during holidays. There was to be no question of any boy considering it a soft option. This is a good rule where service is given as an alternative to some other activity during school time.

At first, eight boys began, with myself, to explore the social needs of the surrounding area. We made early contacts with inner regions of the City of Birmingham where the challenge was more immediately obvious than in prosperous Solihull. These contacts have been maintained ever since. But it soon became clear that on our own doorstep there were needs so considerable that all our energies and as many volunteers as we could muster would be required.

Recruitment within the school grew at such a rate that it became necessary to negotiate with the C.C.F. Commander the number of boys who could be permitted to join the activities on Corps afternoons. A ceiling of seventy volunteers was agreed. As this still left the C.C.F. with over 300 cadets, it was felt that its work would not suffer unduly.

Other boys were, of course, allowed to serve in their own time, and within two years over a hundred volunteers were regularly involved.

The needs were established through the Chief Welfare Officer and the Housing Officer of the County Borough in the first instance. Local voluntary organisations, and particularly the local Society for the Physically Handicapped, also helped. Doctors and district nurses told of people who might be glad of a visit. Other avenues of service were discovered through visits to the matrons and wardens of local institutions. Some of the churches were approached, but it would be true to say that as a route to social need these proved rather disappointing. It was, indeed, not very long before church leaders were seeking information from volunteers as to ways in which their own young people might help. This was encouraging, but it is significant that the Church as an organisation seemed less able to point the way than other voluntary bodies.

During 1963 the enormity of the problem became so evident that several of the boys urged co-operation with other schools. Three of the girls' schools were known already to have engaged in different forms of social service. This, however, was on a small scale, and generally periodic rather than continuous. There was no co-ordination, or attempt to advance on a broad front in serving the community. The pressure for more volunteers grew so intense that action had to be taken. In March 1964 the head boys and girls of five of the leading secondary schools met in Solihull School. Together with some of the main volunteers they signed the Solihull Young Peoples' Charter of Service in the presence of senior members of their schools and adult welfare workers. In this they pledged to work together, and with any other young people who would join them, to meet the needs of their community.

At that meeting the secretary of one church youth fellowship also signed, for it was determined from the first that the work should not be limited to schools alone. It was a deep personal pleasure to me that the young people of my own church joined in so wholeheartedly from the beginning.

From this an organisation of over five hundred young volunteers from twelve secondary schools grew with remarkable rapidity. It is primarily the inspiration of their service that has led to the writing of this book.

Out of their keenness, and awareness of the great needs beyond their own neighbourhood, has grown another large organisation of voluntary service by young people. Their first general secretary, Jane Markham, proved such a dynamic personality and outstanding organiser that she was offered the post of full-time Organising Officer of the Birmingham Young Volunteers' Trust. This offer was made while she was still at school, and she began work only a month after leaving in September 1965.

Her school, known locally as Malvern Hall, the gracious Warwickshire house once painted by Constable, has provided some of our best volunteers, including Maureen, the

General Secretary Elect. The example of Jane has undoubtedly been an inspiration to the girls who have followed her.

The Trust, formed under her leadership, was sponsored by the Solihull Young Volunteers, the Birmingham Association of Youth Clubs, and the Community Service Volunteers, London. This national organisation, led by its founder, Alec Dickson, gave great encouragement to the project from the start. Birmingham Youth Voluntary Service, which at that time ran its own Community Service House for residential volunteers, also sponsored the scheme, and merged itself under Jane Markham's leadership.

Thus it came about that an eighteen year old girl, straight from school, took over the entire management of a city voluntary service scheme for young people. It has already become one of the most successful and vigorous schemes of its kind in the country. Under her inspiration and drive, over a thousand young people within three years have been involved in countless tasks. Fortunately she left Solihull with a worthy successor, but the Birmingham expansion has been so rapid that it has been necessary to find her an assistant of equal dedication and youthful drive.

Yet this, impressive as it is, is only part of a nation-wide movement. With local variations its pattern is repeated in many of our cities and towns, and in rural districts too.

Naturally, this book will be largely a Midland story because this is the one in which I am involved and know at first-hand, but the experiences recounted will be similar to those of volunteers elsewhere.

Some of the work we are doing others may have done before, perhaps better. Although in Solihull we formed one of the first large co-operative schemes in the country we do not claim any pride of place. We are glad to acknowledge that many other young people have served for years as we have. This is precisely why it needs to be written down, for it is a remarkable commentary on modern youth, and shows the possibilities of a breakthrough to meet many pressing social needs of today, not only in this country, but throughout the world.

Recently Elizabeth Hoodless of Community Service Volunteers went to America on a Churchill Fellowship to study the social conditions in that country. There she discovered the diseases of modern civilisation are not just confined to Britain, but are also to be found across the Atlantic. The American internal Peace Corps movement with massive Government support is tackling their incongruous legacy of poverty amidst enormous wealth with an anti-poverty campaign spearheaded by American youth.

When a party of French social workers and youth leaders visited one of the training conferences of our young volunteers they expressed the greatest amazement.

"It is fantastic!" they said, unbelievingly. "In our country young people would not be allowed to help in mental institutions and hospitals. Only professional workers would be permitted there."

But they admitted that their need for young peoples' service on these lines was every bit as real.

Certainly Commonwealth countries have the same real and pressing problems. This was made abundantly clear to me when I recently met the General Secretary of the New Zealand Methodist Youth Department on his fact-finding tour of Britain and America. He showed keen interest in the way many of our young people are responding to the challenge of human needs. He readily agreed that such vital initiative by youth is urgently needed in all countries, including his own. During his world travels he had been impressed by the complex nature of the social problems everywhere, and he appreciated the need for youth to step in to the rescue. International Voluntary Service, Toc H and similar organisations have proved conclusively through their work camps in Europe and other parts of the world, how widespread are these human needs. Yet, despite this universality of social distress, whether in city or village, we must all start where we are now.

To young volunteers everywhere my story will have a familiar ring. "But this is our story, too," they will say.

And so it is.

Chapter 2

THE INVOLVEMENT OF YOUNG PEOPLE

THE OLD LADY lived in squalor. I remember first taking boys to visit her in the tiny downstairs room. Outside the window the heavy stream of traffic rumbled by. All day long its busy roar penetrated the thin walls of that little terraced house. But she was in a world apart. It was a squalid world. It smelt. And it was filthy.

Yet there was a certain distinction about her. She spoke in a cultured manner. She must have been a fine-looking woman in her day. Her carefully brushed hair lay softly on her shoulders as she sat propped up in bed. Although she was very old the wrinkles on her face were not harsh or deep. But she could no longer cope with life on her own. Yet, with resolution and cunning she had defied all the efforts of social workers to persuade her to go into a Home. This was her little bit of world. She was afraid to let it go.

No adult voluntary organisation would continue to serve her; the conditions were regarded as too unhygienic. So the young volunteers took over. Somebody had to. They realised that in her state she could not be left to fend alone. Apart from neighbours almost as old as she was, no one else had helped her regularly in the three years that elapsed before she was moved compulsorily into a hospital geriatric ward.

Although she was virtually bed-ridden she could have

done more for herself; but her mind wandered, and she had ceased to care. Her standards had gone long ago. She did not even bother to drag herself to the outside lavatory which was not far away. A large pail inside the room served instead. The boys emptied it for her. They called three or four times a week. She rarely did any washing up. Many a volunteer spent most of his visit in the gloomy scullery scraping the dried-up leavings of several meals from dirty plates.

Every so often a grand descent was made upon the room and the adjoining scullery. The mess and refuse were all cleared away. But within a few days things were as bad again. It seemed a hopeless struggle. Girls, too, played their part, but with no more success.

Was it worthwhile? I believe so. The boys and girls felt sure it was. They did not enjoy what they had to do, but they made allowances. They knew the infirmity of her mind. She did not remember their names from one visit to the next, or even that they had been before, but she was pathetically pleased to see them.

They did her shopping and fetched her pension. One boy fitted up a radio for her. One of her happiest moments was when volunteers came and filled her room with flowers after a Harvest Festival. Her face lit up whenever they came and they knew their visits did her good. When, eventually, she was taken into hospital she did not last long.

What was the secret of their dedication? Why did they keep it up so determinedly? They had become involved. This involvement of young people in service to others is one of the most hopeful signs of our age.

Yet it does not happen by accident. The upsurge of social concern among young people may seem to be spontaneous.

But interest has first to be aroused. Opportunities must be sought, and for this the right kind of positive adult leadership is essential.

An experienced youth leader or teacher has a considerable advantage, but personality enters into it. He must be vigorous and young in spirit. He must be able to communicate a sense of social urgency. But he must not push youngsters around. This will not involve them. They will not stand for it.

Jane Markham first hit the newspaper headlines when still at school. She had forthrightly told an adult organiser of social work, the main speaker at a city conference, "Youth won't be led by the nose."

She was quite right. Having been well trained by her in the first place, I would not dare to direct my secretaries as to what they should and should not do.

Her successor, John, is even more adamant, and extremely thorough and efficient. With the help of his deputy and the other secretaries he has shown administrative ability of a high order. If he suspected for a moment that I was attempting to interfere with policy planning he would undoubtedly be upset. This is as it should be. But the secretaries are all very tolerant with me. They listen with infinite patience and politeness to any advice I may have to offer, and sometimes even act upon it. Usually I try to be wise enough to wait until they ask for advice before I offer it. This can be hard on a person of my temperament. Such self-effacement, I suppose, is good for my soul. I am sure it is good for the movement.

Yet the approach of an adult adviser is bound to vary somewhat according to the age-range of the volunteers. The leaders of my own group are largely drawn from the pre-university year of school, but elsewhere they are younger. We must always be prepared to consider a question often asked—"How young may a young volunteer be?"

Dr. E. L. M. Millar, Chief Medical Officer of Health for the City of Birmingham, said at a recent conference on youth voluntary service that no one is too young to begin. Even babies could do it. He cited as an example the great value to mentally backward babies and toddlers of having normally endowed children to play with them. This was a timely reminder to a conference considering the place of the teenager in community service. The very young can serve usefully, entertain, show compassion, respond to need or give delight with the rest of us. Anyone who has seen the real pleasure given to the elderly by an entertainment specially put on for them in an infant school knows this only too well.

I took a group of bell ringers round the geriatric wards of the local hospital at Christmas. They were only young boys, not one more than eleven years of age, yet the delight caused by their fresh shining faces and lively spirits, not to mention the carols they rang out, was obvious. We might pause to ask ourselves at what age we were most successful with our grandmothers.

Without doubt the time will come when the splendid work done in so many primary schools in enlisting the enthusiasm of juniors in active service is more fully recognised.

Yet, for widely planned service, maintained over long periods of time and organised on a large scale, it is the secondary stage of schooling to which we shall turn. Volunteers below or above this age-range may be linked to, or supplement, what is being done but will not fundamentally alter its content or pattern.

There are two main ways in which a leader may actively involve his youngsters. He can introduce them to specific needs which he has carefully sought out beforehand. The old lady was a good example of this. I simply took boys from school to see her one day. They were so shocked to find anyone living in such conditions within a few hundred yards of the school that they immediately resolved to adopt her. Before that day was over they were in action. Similarly, when girls were needed to supplement what the boys had begun I introduced two from my church youth fellowship. There was no need to do more. Once young people meet someone like that they rise splendidly to the occasion.

Alternatively, a teacher or club leader may arouse interest through discussion groups. In school this may be a part of a civic or religious education programme. This gives the teacher of scripture a wonderful opportunity to make Christianity relevant today. The creeds of young people must be written in deeds, not words. It should be so for us all. I use my own lessons quite freely to invoke social conscience and commitment.

This awakening of a sense of concern for others is a most important preliminary. It can be disastrous to throw young volunteers into action before they are really concerned. I know of one youth club leader who undertook a large task of interior decoration with his club. But their heart was not in it. To them it was a bit of a lark. They soon tired. The job dragged on for six weeks and was badly done. The leader ended up by doing it himself. He made a good job of it, but this is really failure. The leader's task is not to do his volunteers' work for them. Before he commits youngsters to voluntary work or begins a scheme of service he must discover ways of rousing their social concern.

Sometimes organisers have tried to do this by carrying out a social survey of the area. Questionnaires have been sent out, and a great deal of interesting information accu-

THE INVOLVEMENT OF YOUNG PEOPLE

mulated. The school or youth group concerned has then been able to plan ways of meeting the social needs disclosed.

In one large city this was done on a vast scale. The whole city was divided into districts. Many youth groups were enlisted to deliver and collect the questionnaires, but when all this had been done, considerable difficulty was experienced. The organisers found they had aroused far more hopes than they had the volunteers to satisfy. Enthusiastic central planning had overlooked the vital necessity of maintaining enthusiasm in local regions, or of ensuring that regular volunteers were available in sufficient numbers. Much disappointment was caused that could have been avoided.

Social surveys have their appeal in an age that loves its neatly tabulated statistical information. I do not doubt that much that is useful can be learned from them. It must never be forgotten, however, that old and handicapped people are more interested in a boy or girl turning up on their doorstep, prepared to do a practical job of work. They have probably developed a healthy cynicism towards filling forms.

Of course, it is important to have an accurate assessment of local need, but there are other ways of obtaining this, as I have already indicated.

More important and valuable than carrying out grand surveys is the discovery of the springs of action that cause young people to respond.

Chapter 3

THE SPRINGS OF ACTION

A T ROOT WE ARE SEEKING a religious response. The indignant protests of humanists seem to rise up round me as I write. But it is true. The springs of action are deeply religious in the best sense of that word. Of course, I do not mean for one moment that every volunteer is a professing Christian. Nor do I suggest that service must be tied to doctrine. After all, the Good Samaritan was not a professing Jew, yet he was commended by the Son of God. Why? Was it not precisely because Jesus wished to show that true religion is a matter of deeds, not words? His whole life was a call to men to be doers of the word and not hearers only.

The story He told of the separation of the sheep from the goats at the Last Day drives home the message. Nothing is more apt for a volunteer. For what is the criterion of judgment given? Is it not simply how we have responded to those in need? Have we fed the hungry, given welcome to the stranger, clothed the naked, and visited the sick?

"Inasmuch as you have done it to the least of these you have done it to me."

Non-Christian volunteers may yet share the surprise shown by the people being judged in this parable. Professing Christians who sit comfortably in their pews each Sunday, and do nothing about it during the week, may also have their surprises.

Voluntary service touches the vital emotion of Christi-

anity. Caring love is its mainspring. Not in any weak senti-
mental sense, but with that deep concern that Christ Himself showed.

What we are asking of youth is a response of practical
sympathy for their fellows, issuing in positive action. We
are asking them to take upon their strong shoulders the
burdens of the weak and old, the helpless and the deprived.
If that is not Christianity God alone knows what it is!

This being so, it is a cause for serious reflection on the
part of church leaders that a movement of such vitality and
compassion in Britain today should be so often in origin
and organisation outside the framework of the Christian
Youth Service. There are, of course, many Youth Organisations within the Church which have played leading roles
in fostering a spirit of service, but in the breadth and
imagination of recent developments there is a danger of
the churches being left behind.

This is not meant to be a criticism of Christian Youth
leaders; I am one myself. However, although our failure to
involve church youngsters as fully as we might is not due
only to apathy or lack of imagination, these have undoubtedly been contributory factors. Because large schemes
of co-operative voluntary service are so recent there is a
natural dearth of experienced organisers. This makes it
difficult for the heads of youth organisations to provide the
guidance and inspiration needed at local level.

Here is an important area in which all Christians can
combine wholeheartedly with those outside the Church.
Credal and doctrinal differences are of no account for it is
here that the true ecumenical spirit can be lived out pur-
posefully. As the Rev. Ernest Marvin of Bristol, author of
that arresting play, *A Man Dies*, so rightly remarked,
"Labels put youngsters off, but they respond to need when

they are shown it."

In a recent TV Religious programme we heard of a mini-skirted teenager who sat down in a pew and said to her middle-aged neighbour, "It's bloody 'ot in 'ere!" Shocked, her neighbour walked out of the service. It is not likely that such teenagers will be seen in our churches unless we involve them in deeds which prove that our faith has meaning. Though I do not for a moment underestimate the place of worship, I believe they will find the true Christ more readily in helping a crippled old lady than they will with a sermon on Christian ethics.

This is why it is so important for us to encourage our church youngsters to serve alongside those outside the Church. We should not be afraid to enlist the help of existing organisations and work with them. The churches undoubtedly have a splendid record in raising volunteers for service overseas and within their own organisations, but it is on the home front, outside the church doors, that we often do not appear to have involved our youngsters imaginatively enough.

Yet this need not be so. The centre of many of our own activities is a Methodist church hall. The councils of secretaries and gatherings of volunteers are held in it. The Physically Handicapped Youth Club also meets there regularly, and church members help with transport. The local Congregational Church holds special services for the handicapped in which young volunteers help. We invited one hundred and thirty old people to a Harvest Festival service in the school chapel. There they were welcomed by as many volunteers from several of the borough's secondary schools. Afterwards they were given refreshments and harvest gifts prepared by the boys and girls. The headmaster then spoke to each old person in turn. He presented them all with a photograph of the chapel altar and mural.

Another service was held, again with the co-operation of volunteers, for sufferers from muscular dystrophy. In many similar ways the school chapel is becoming a centre of involvement with real-life problems. This is vital if school religion is to earn and keep the respect of the boys. It is essential for any church if it is to survive.

Many young folk are alienated from the Church because they feel it is out of touch with the things that really matter. Yet the influence of a young person of Christian principles and outlook can add a quality and sense of direction to much voluntary work. It would be a poor reflection on Christian heritage if the Church allowed itself to be outshone in good works. This is surely one of its great opportunities; not to assert dogma or make converts, but to plunge wholeheartedly into a movement where the spiritual realities it stands for are being expressed in such practical form by the rising generation. If, without denominational bias, the Church were to do this it would make a greater impact upon society than at present.

A non-churchgoing volunteer once paid a sincere tribute to the secretary of her school group of over a hundred members. She said she was sure the other girls had chosen her because she was such a good Christian. When a tribute like that is paid in an age generally acknowledged to be one of disbelief, the possibilities for Christian witness in the field of youth voluntary service are obvious.

The girl referred to happens to be one of the young teachers of the Methodist Junior Church of which I am the General Superintendent. For two years she has willingly given up her weekends to care for deprived children from a Reception Home. Apart from her responsibilities as a leader, she has also helped elderly and handicapped people.

But she and others like her do not regard such work as an irksome duty. They are happy to do it. There are two hundred and fifty children and young people in this Junior Church and I am naturally delighted at the response so many of them give to, and their influence upon, the whole movement. I have no say in their selection as community service leaders. They are chosen by their fellows in their different schools. Yet it is remarkable how many of these Christian youngsters are selected for the highest positions.

No distinction, of course, is made between Christian volunteers and others. Those who belong to a church would be most embarrassed and indignant if there were. They value too highly the contributions of others, and admire the fact that they are prepared to help without any basis of Christian belief. Yet it is wholly good that the Church should be seen to be actively involved, and that its young people should take a leading part.

Voluntary work by young people was once the theme of an interesting discussion during a special form of Sunday worship at my church. It was agreed that the quality of service given did not depend upon the particular beliefs of the volunteer. Yet it was felt that Christian service should have an extra dimension, perhaps only apparent in moments of crisis or death, which is part of the nature of the faith. This makes it important for Christians to permeate community service at every level.

Adult church members have a special responsibility to young people here. We must show them that the Church is alive. Youth responds to vitality, and the Christian Church should be alert to the needs of society. If we present young people with a caring Church they will be glad to demonstrate their faith by helping others, alongside those who do not necessarily share their beliefs.

Chapter 4

NEEDS REAL AND UNREAL

S HE WAS DEAD. She'd died two years ago," said the young volunteer in scarcely disguised tones of disgust. He was reporting on his first job. The disgust was justified. There is no excuse for inadequate exploration of need, or for presenting volunteers with out-of-date addresses. Nothing can lead more rapidly to disillusionment, or more certainly throw the work into disrepute.

Two boys once went to offer their services at a particular address. They were told that the house and garden were in unkempt condition, and that the elderly gentleman living there would appreciate help. As they walked up the smooth-surfaced drive to the smart front door of an immaculate home, they knew something must be wrong. This was, however, the address they had been given, so they rang the bell, hopefully. A retired military gentleman of high rank answered the door. When they had stammered out the purpose of their visit he reddened noticeably. "Social service!" he barked. "Do I look as though I need social service?" The door was slammed, and two crestfallen volunteers returned to base only to learn that they had been given the wrong number.

An organiser is dependent to some extent on lists of addresses given to him by other people or organisations. Even so he should, before sending volunteers, check them himself wherever possible. Sometimes, when a genuine address has been found, the need does not seem challenging enough.

Old people are not always imaginative in their use of volunteers but need to be guided with suggestions as to the kinds of service that can be done. It is frustrating for a volunteer to be told there is nothing to do after he has cycled several miles to help. He must, however, also be prepared to use his imagination. Not all, perhaps, would show the cool nerve of one boy who went to visit an old lady after a very hard day at school. He confessed afterwards, "She was tired and I was tired, so we both went to sleep." Close understanding was achieved between them from that day on.

Volunteers must not despise routine work. The ordinary little jobs that seem unexciting mean a great deal to the elderly or handicapped. Sometimes all they want is someone to talk to. Two of our girls once set off enthusiastically to make their first call but they arrived too late. The elderly lady had gassed herself out of sheer loneliness the week before.

One boy was asked to make a bed-table for an old lady he visited regularly. He took this request to the school woodwork shop where, because of pressure of other work, it took several weeks to finish. At last it was ready. He carried it triumphantly to her home. He knew how much she had been looking forward to it. She had asked about it so often. But he, also, was too late. She had died of cancer only a day or two previously.

There is an urgency about the ordinary tasks we are asked to do. Sometimes volunteers have to learn this the hard way.

All the same, young volunteers want real jobs. In one of Alec Dickson's favourite quotations from a letter he received from a volunteer are the words, "It's not blood we're afraid of, it's boredom."

Some needs cry out more desperately than others. In Balsall Heath many old people live in appalling conditions while they wait for a place in the new blocks of flats rising round them. Meanwhile we send in teams of volunteers to give what help they can.

One old lady lived in abject loneliness in a small room on the first floor of a large Victorian residence which had been converted into flats. She was shamefully exploited by other people living there. This is not unusual. When such old people depend on others to do their shopping, or prepare meals, they are sometimes forced to pay excessively. If they cannot manage their own finances very well, money is easily extracted from them. Often they are so frightened of other people in the house or nearby that they dare not resist ill-meaning gestures.

Martin, a police cadet volunteer, was sent to help. He did a wonderful job for her and for other old people. He was supported by teams of volunteers from Solihull School and King Edward's School. The smell pervaded everywhere. As one boy said, "Filth clung to you like treacle." Empty beer bottles rolled round the floor beneath the old double bed which almost filled the room, for she had become an alcoholic. Although we could never accuse any of the other occupants in particular, they were always ready to blame each other.

It was clear that someone was satisfying her craving for drink at the expense of her small hoard of savings and personal effects. The boys decorated her room. Volunteers collected her pension and did her shopping as often as possible. Unfortunately others had the advantage of being on the spot all the time.

Eventually the place began to look fit to live in. But by now she was too ill to be left there any longer. Today she is in hospital, almost certainly too sick ever to return. Her room has since been ransacked by neighbours.

The Welfare Officer in charge of voluntary service for the elderly in Balsall Heath writes, "At the end it was like a descent of vultures. All was taken and when we arrived— nothing remained but an empty, filthy room."

So often people assume that these things cannot be. Somehow they mistakenly believe such problems are covered by the Welfare State. It is not generally realised how many gaps still remain which can only be filled by voluntary effort. The younger generation, certainly, is not impressed by what it sees of the Welfare State. It was a bad day when that misleading phrase was first invented. Far too many consciences have lain undisturbed because of a vague belief that the State is doing it all. Only in comparatively recent days have T.V. programmes like Jeremy Sandford's *Cathy come Home* and books like Canon Norman Power's *Forgotten People* begun to shatter illusions.

I have before me a letter written by a frustrated welfare worker of considerable experience. The following extract tells of the difficulties often faced when trying to get statutory help for old people: "We were very disappointed with the local authorities who seemed to do little or nothing really to help. So often we get desperate and have to make impassioned pleas, followed by threats to expose the situation to the national newspapers."

The letter goes on to tell of a very old lady suddenly unable to cope because of mental difficulties. Her doctor was asked to assess her need to be placed in an old people's home. He became very cross and shouted angrily, but refused to help. The local authorities did nothing when first approached, and it was only after the extreme danger had again been pointed out that any action was taken.

Another tragic incident concerned a patient sent home prematurely from a mental hospital. The problem was not resolved until the welfare worker had demanded to put the matter before the chief medical officer.

Such crises are sometimes solved only by the intervention of a voluntary organisation. As the quoted letter concludes: "The statutory bodies have too much work to do. All our old folk are our friends and not just case work; thus we must help them all we can."

These words reveal a very unsatisfactory situation. I believe it important that the problems they indicate should be more widely appreciated.

In Solihull I have every reason to be grateful for the encouragement given by local authorities to the development of service by the young. It is obvious their work is greatly welcomed. In Birmingham, too, the Health and Welfare Departments have used their services enthusiastically. It is fully accepted that there exists a vast field of social need in which young people have a most valuable contribution to make. Often it is a contribution which cannot be made by anyone else.

This fact was brought home to me when the local Red Cross made an emergency appeal to our Group at the end of term. All at once five handicapped people found themselves in desperate need of "Home Helps" because of a temporary collapse of the local organisation. This meant finding a daily rota of volunteers for over a fortnight. No other local agency could meet this emergency. Margaret, Acting General Secretary, coped with the crisis magnificently and without fuss. Within twenty-four hours all the

emergencies had been met by a team of young helpers wh
shouldered the unexpected tasks until the crisis was ove

This is typical of Margaret, a most attractive girl, whos
natural charm conceals an unexpected ability to lead an
organise, but she would be the first to pass the credit t
those who respond to her call. When she addressed a cor
ference at Ipswich she hinted at the secret of her Group
enthusiasm. "In our Council meetings," she said, "we d
our own planning and say what we like. No adult tells u
what we should do."

We have seen how youngsters find some needs uncor
vincing. Others do not materialise as they expect. On
volunteer took a blind lady's dog out for a walk. She con
plained repeatedly of how hard life had become for he
since she went blind.

On the way back to her house the boy had trouble with
the dog which refused to budge. So he picked it up an
carried it home. The blind lady opened the door to him
indignantly.

"How dare you carry my dog?" she said, sharply. "Tak
him back and give him a proper walk."

When the boy had recovered from his surprise, and th
slight cynicism which this incident produced, he turned hi
attention to another form of service. He has now repaired
almost fifty "Talking Books" for people who are *totally*
blind.

Yet many services, which appear to be routine, revea
unimagined depths. We have seen, too, how shocking som
situations are to those who come into close contact with
them.

Lord Ritchie Calder, Chairman of the Edinburgh
University Fellowship, recently made the point in a B.B.C
broadcast that the nation should offer youngsters *Adven*

ure with a Purpose. This is true, for youth needs and will
espond to a challenge. Unaware of the fear and poverty of
he 1930s, which still colour the attitudes of adults, they do
ot seek a "Welfare State" but a "Fulfilment State". It is up
o the adult world to lead them to the needs which exist in
very neighbourhood. *Adventure with a Purpose* could
be a call to greater recognition of what life is really about,
ince in responding to the needs of others youngsters may
ind both the adventure and purpose for which they are
orever seeking.

A most striking example of this is Sally Trench, a
London J.P.'s twenty-two-year-old daughter, who has lived
or two years among East End "meths" drinkers, trying to
help them overcome their desperate problems. Her booklet
on this work, published by the Simon Community Trust
through which she has served, shows how great are their
needs. She has given up her friends in order to help them
and has begged money and food to keep many of them
alive. Her own magnificent response to need shows what
young people are capable of when confronted with challenges which they recognise as urgent and real. But
whether the needs are mundane or desperate they will
always do their best to meet them once they are convinced
they are genuine. It only remains for adults to encourage
and give them the opportunities to serve.

Chapter 5

BREAKING DOWN THE BARRIERS

THE LUXURY GOLF CLUB is flanked on one side by houses so splendid that the road is popularly nicknamed "Millionaires' Row." Just beyond it, set back from the main road, is a rather unpretentious line of small dwellings. In one of these the old folk lived in the back scullery. They must have chosen the scullery because it was the only place in which they could keep warm. Certainly the rest of the house was not fit to live in. Neither was the scullery, but they lived there.

They had cheated death for at least a decade; the woman particularly. They were both well over ninety, but it was not the years that mattered. I have never met anyone so ancient as that woman. Her wizened face was crumpled with deep wrinkles. When she groped across the room—she was virtually blind—we never knew how she would reach the door. It was only a few feet away, but she shuffled inches at a time. She drew her breath in deep gasps.

The husband was not so helpless. Certainly he understood what was happening more than she did. But he was beyond helping her.

The Welfare Officer had asked us to decorate the place, but warned they might be hostile and difficult. I inspected the project. It was foul. The ceiling and walls were quite black, but we were not without experience of such conditions. The smell was just one of the occupational hazards of the volunteer. So the boys were sent in to tackle the job.

Then came the phone call. I can hear now the anxious tones of the boy at the other end.

"Sir, what shall we do? We've stripped off some of the wallpaper and the walls are crawling with lice."

There was now only one possible course of action. The sanitary inspector was called. The room was fumigated. It was not quite as bad as the boy had thought. The lice he had reported turned out to be wood-lice.

The ancient lino that had to be lifted was so brittle that it crumbled away, revealing a bare, cold, uneven brick floor. The subdued hostility of the old couple flared into incoherent fury. The young decorators were sent packing. The barrier became complete. Matters could hardly be worse. One seventeen years old boy became so emotionally upset at the state in which the old couple were living, and what he felt was the total adult indifference to their plight, that he wept unashamedly. The problem had suddenly become a major crisis for the group. There was to my mind only one thing to be done. We must send for Scott.

David Scott was a Solihull School boarder. He remains in many ways the most remarkable volunteer we have had. To look at he was small and not very imposing, but his personality was outstanding. He had an acute perception of what any situation required, and a delightful sense of humour in dealing with it. What was, in this instance, much to the point, he had an uncanny knack of dealing with old people. No boy was better able to handle a difficult situation.

I caught him as he was entering the boarding house. Within minutes I had rushed him to the crisis spot. The situation was still explosive. Volunteers sat disconsolately on buckets outside the back door. With unabashed cowardice we pushed David inside. Then we waited. The minutes ticked by. I felt like an expectant father as I paced up and down in the back yard. Had I been a smoker the ground would have been littered with cigarette ends.

Suddenly an unusual cackling sound came from within. We dared to peep through the window. There was David eating cake and drinking tea with the old couple. They were chortling away as if they were hearing the jokes of the century. I shall never quite know how he achieved it, but then we did not care. The barriers were down. The work could go on.

From then on the boarders took over. They were outraged by the whole situation, and determined to do something about it. Apart from the decorating, they pulled a trek-cart load of timber two miles to the house. This they had begged from a demolition site. They worked in shifts to chop it all up. A massive fuel supply was soon provided. Later volunteers delivered coal. Meanwhile the room was being transformed.

In the middle of the job David's indignation got the better of him. He marched up one of the long drives in "Millionaires' Row" to a particularly fine house. Splattered with paint and rather dishevelled, he asked the surprised lady who answered the door if she really knew how her neighbours were living. Since she would not believe him he insisted on showing her.

At last the job was finished. An appeal to a local church produced a carpet. It was just the right size. For the remaining months of their lives the old couple had something soft and warm to walk on. They also had the constant companionship of young volunteers. When in the end they died within a few days of each other they knew someone had cared.

Stories of David's flair for handling the elderly are not easily forgotten. One was related to me more than two years afterwards by a volunteer who had found an old lady particularly hard to please. She was thoughtlessly critical of everything he did. When he wrote letters for her she dictated them too fast and then blamed him for not keeping up. When she gave him jobs to do she was never satisfied with his efforts though he did his best. He had reached the point where he felt he could not endure it much longer when David arrived unexpectedly. It took him a very short time to assess the situation. He spoke frankly to the lady.

"You ought not to treat your volunteer like this," he said, in a reproving tone. "He's come to help you, you know. If you're not careful, you'll lose him."

The harassed volunteer was stunned by David's nerve.

"I was scared to death," he told me as he related the incident. "I didn't know what she would do, but the funny thing is she became as meek as a lamb and I never had any more trouble with her."

David's genius for breaking down barriers was not confined to old people. Once he had to open up the possibilities of service for volunteers in a large mental hospital. It was hard going. Even his uninhibited gaiety and willingness to chat produced no result. The patients sat round the room staring at him stolidly, but making no response. Almost in despair he thumped his hand down upon the large table. One of the men then slowly rose from his seat, and to David's surprise, copied him. In a flash he knew what he must do. Before long he was the leader of a rhythmic tattoo being beaten out upon the table by delighted patients. He had broken through.

Usually with old people the barriers that exist are those of pride, independence and even suspicion. They have to be made to realise that they are helping the volunteers. An appeal for their support on these lines makes all the difference. It is a sincere appeal, for they have much to give to a young person. Their experience of life and the ways in which they have learned to face its realities are benefits that only they can pass on. Just by being able to offer opportunities of service they help youngsters to learn about life and find a sense of purpose and achievement.

Once an old person understands this a young volunteer can make a break through which is almost impossible for most adults. The elderly often regard adult social workers with suspicion and resentment. They feel patronised even when they are not. Sometimes they suspect the adult of secretly plotting to get them into a Home, or being in league with the authorities. With a youngster they feel much more at ease.

I once had an excellent example of this. I went with a volunteer to visit a blind and extremely deaf old man who was sitting up in bed with a night cap on, cheerfully awaiting his young visitor. When John, the volunteer, tried to introduce me the atmosphere immediately froze. After a long pause he demanded to know my age. Somewhat embarrassed, I had to shout this out very loudly several times before he acknowledged that he had heard. He then ignored me completely, and directed all his attention to John, who after months of patience and determination had gained the old man's entire confidence.

My cup of humility was full when, as I departed, he burst out singing sea-shanties, so delighted was he to realise that he was alone with his young volunteer.

Sometimes there are barriers to be broken in Old

Peoples' Homes and hospitals. Matrons imaginative enough to think out in advance ways in which young people may help are an enormous asset. I have known many. They are valuable allies. They gain the loyal support and enthusiasm of volunteers. Their rewards are tangible, and the institution springs to life with youth voluntary service. Others, however, are less co-operative. Some matrons are afraid to let youngsters near their residents. They feel the limit has been reached when the volunteer has been given a hoe and shown a border full of weeds. In such instances the only hope lies in a full and frank interview. The organiser should point out what he is trying to achieve for his volunteers as well as for the residents. Sometimes even this fails.

We had a large number of girls keen to serve in a Children's Home. When they arrived almost the only work they were asked to do was the washing up and ironing. They hardly ever saw the children they had come to help. This was not good enough. The girls did not object to hard work, but they resented being used as free domestic labour. If only we could have persuaded the matron to balance their work by letting them help with the children as well she would have their services today. In another Children's Home where a different attitude prevailed, over thirty volunteers help throughout each week. They do much domestic work very willingly; but it has not been forgotten that they have come primarily to help with the children.

The last major area where barriers may have to be broken down is in the existing organisation of voluntary service within a district. This is particularly true where service by the young is considered an innovation. I must admit that my personal experience in my own district has been most fortunate, but it is not always so elsewhere, particularly where the organisational pattern of service in a neighbourhood has become fixed.

Where there are already vested interests and petty jealousies between voluntary agencies, an adult leader may have to help his volunteers considerably. His experience and maturity of judgment will be invaluable to them. It would be surprising if the infusion of new youthful energies and ideas did not arouse some opposition.

Difficulties are made to be overcome. They present a challenge, particularly to young people. Much of human history is concerned with overcoming obstacles to a coveted goal. Whether or not that goal is the conquest of Everest, a landing on the moon, or sailing round the world single-handed, man moves towards it with stubborn determination. The tumultuous welcome Sir Francis Chichester received when he sailed into Plymouth Harbour at the end of his long and lonely voyage was remarkable for the great numbers of children and teenagers who turned out to greet him. Their spontaneous tribute to this courageous man showed how little age counts when they recognise a genuinely youthful spirit and determination. For youngsters themselves there is added to such determination a vitality and impatience for immediate action. Their sense of urgency can be successful in removing barriers which might delay more cautious elders for a considerably longer period.

Chapter 6

HELPING THE DEAF, DUMB AND BLIND

THE SILENCE was profound and uncanny. It is not possible to imagine what such total isolation must be like. I hoped fervently that the volunteers would have more idea of what to do than I had. We entered that very ordinary lounge to meet a situation more extraordinary than any we had yet faced, for the other occupants, seated here and there round the room, were wholly unaware of our existence. The void surrounding them was absolute. They were deaf, dumb and blind. How could anyone know such emptiness and still want to live?

I looked at the boys anxiously. What had I let them in for? Matron had simply thrust the manual language chart in our hands and left us to it. She gave the impression of being almost too busy to cope with volunteers. The boys had wanted to be confronted with a new kind of challenge. Well, they could not complain. I had found them one. The experience of entering a home in which several residents are afflicted with this triple handicap is as daunting a challenge as any young volunteer is likely to face. One of the boys glanced at me enquiringly.

"What'll I do?" he whispered, forgetting there was no need to be quiet.

I shrugged my shoulders, helplessly.

"You'll have to try to make contact with one of them," I

said, thankful in a cowardly sort of way that I believed in giving youngsters full responsibility.

He coughed nervously and gripped his manual chart a little tighter. Then he stepped across the room hesitantly. An old lady sat before him, her head nodding, and her lips moving silently to no purpose. He touched her sleeve. The effect was startling. A sudden smile broke the vacancy of her expression. She stretched out a trembling, anxious hand. She was searching desperately for a contact.

The boy took her hand. Very slowly he began to spell out his message from the manual chart. She nodded eagerly to show she understood. Someone, she could not possibly understand who, was trying to communicate with her. The whole scene was very moving.

This was the start of our work in a Home for the blind, deaf and dumb. We regard it today as one of our toughest assignments, for it is often emotionally exhausting. Girls from our group at Olton Court Convent School are serving there at present.

Once, the boys were more than startled when a resident threw an angry fit. With strange, pathetic sounds of inarticulate rage she threw herself about and beat the wall with clenched fists. The incident awed them. She was quickly led away, but they had glimpsed a bitter frustration they would never forget.

Not all the residents suffer three handicaps. Some have only two, or even one. Communication with them is not so hard.

The boys managed to get through to one resident who was almost blind, and also deaf. They used a large scribbling pad and wrote in huge block letters that would have been adequate for most hoardings! It worked. A lively, if rather slow conversation developed. Another volunteer encouraged a blind lady to teach him Braille. The lessons had to be short as she was old, and tired easily, but the principle was sound. She was helping the volunteer. Her life had a new purpose.

One boy visited a blind man in his own private flat. He discovered that the man's great interests were tape-recording and motor racing. He encouraged these interests as much as possible and learned a considerable amount of technical detail. The man had the pleasure of teaching the boy something about subjects in which he was an expert.

The independence of most blind people, and their ability to cope, are among the earliest discoveries of volunteers who help them. Yet there is still much that can be done. Sometimes the requests are unusual. One boy had to write a letter of complaint to the Prime Minister of the day on his blind lady's behalf. He even had the pleasure of reading her the reply. From time to time she asks him to take her into the main street so that she can stand there with a collection tin for the R.S.P.C.A., for she is fond of animals. This is one occasion when we waive our rule not to become involved in flag days or charity collections.

Another blind lady takes her volunteers for long walks beside the canal. They thought at first that they were going to take her, but after many marathon outings they are no longer under such an illusion. She is a young person, full of spirit, and keeps her home spotless. When we took the Mayor to visit her he was amazed by the carefully arranged flowers and well-polished furniture.

We have no schools for blind children near to us in Solihull, but young volunteers in other parts of the country do good work in such schools, visiting the children and taking them for walks.

I recall my fascination when I first witnessed blind

children playing cricket, using soft cane balls with tin foil inside. They bowled, batted and fielded with an accuracy that would have done credit to an ordinary team. Nearby a group of infants, blind from birth, played hide and seek. The irony of the situation struck me forcibly at the time. Volunteers who join in such games might find their blind team-mates on the spot before them.

Some of our boys play chess during the holidays with a blind boy, home from boarding school. As every chess player knows, the companionship which develops with the game means as much as the game itself.

Any visitor of the deaf, dumb or blind, must use imaginatively whatever aids are at his disposal. For the deaf and dumb the visual aid is his great ally. Coloured slides of holidays abroad, with suitable clear captions, go down well. Family snapshots and films are popular, too, and help the handicapped and their volunteers to get to know each other better. I know from experience that even blind people need not be left out when these are being shown. This was revealed to me particularly in the case of one member of our physically handicapped club who is going blind. She stopped coming for a while, partly because she felt unable to join in the activities. The fellowship had meant so much to her that we could not allow her to drift away. So a special effort is now being made to help her feel at home again. When there are film evenings, volunteers sit beside her, filling in the background details. The last film was a good comedy, and this help enabled her to enjoy it with the rest. We have decided as a result of this success to invite other blind youngsters to join the club.

Once this same girl delightedly showed us a snapshot of herself. "Look," she said, proudly, holding it out to us, "this is a photo of me, presenting a bouquet to the

Mayoress." We expressed our surprise and delight. It was a good photograph, taken during her recent stay at a Cheshire Home in a neighbouring town. She will never be able to see it, but it meant a great deal to her and was a point of contact.

It is important to share interests and hobbies. One of our boys specialised in puppet shows, and had a splendid model theatre. It did not matter that many of the old people to whom he showed them were too deaf to hear all that was going on. They still enjoyed what they saw.

The volunteer who first thought of taking a blind boy for rides on a tandem showed real imagination. His passenger was thrilled by the feel of the wind on his face as they sped down the hills. We have not yet done this in Solihull, but I hope one day we shall.

Hobbies and interests shared with blind people naturally depend largely on what can be heard or felt. One blind lady wins prizes in cookery and craftwork competitions. Her hard work and effort are more than compensated for by the satisfaction and sense of achievement she feels.

"You know," she said to me one day when I was visiting her, "your young volunteers ought to do a tape recording for the blind."

So we did one. A group of volunteers gathered at my home. I asked her to interview the boys and girls on their work and this presented no difficulty to her. I knew that she had once interviewed the captain of the *Queen Elizabeth* without turning a hair.

A girl strummed on her guitar, and sang a comic folk song about a worm. One of the boys played the clarinet. Other boys and girls told of their experiences in voluntary service. Even I was roped in, to recount my most amusing moment. I told how once a very tall and impressive colleague of mine agreed to act the part of Goliath in a play with a cast of thirty young boys. At the first rehearsal he gave such a mighty giant's roar that his false teeth shot out. The boys were so convulsed with mirth that it was ten minutes before the rehearsal could be resumed, but he was a good sport and after having recovered his denture carried on as if nothing had happened.

The recording was great fun. We did not try to be too professional. The tape has since been enjoyed by blind people all over the country.

This lady is in many ways the most remarkable blind person we visit. She has real courage and an unquenchable spirit, and does her volunteers far more good than they do her. Girls go to her each week and address her postcards and letters, and help her in the house. The boys go shopping with her, chop her firewood, and work in the garden as well as indoors. She shows such a lively personal interest in them all that they love to go. When they leave school and go on to university they keep in touch with her. She receives many interesting letters from them. She has been blind for over twenty-five years, and has recently lost her husband. We invited her to address one of our general meetings of volunteers. It was then that the boys realised how important it is to explain to a blind person exactly what are their surroundings.

As the volunteer led her to the front of a large modern school hall, she tightened her grip upon his arm, and attracted his attention. She spoke softly to avoid being overheard, for the hum of noise told her that many volunteers were already seated in the hall.

"Tell me," she said, "exactly what this hall is like. Remember, to me it's just voices in the dark."

We tried to describe the scene, where we were going to

sit, and what was in front of her. She was relieved to know
that there was a table, for she liked to be able to touch
something solid while she was speaking. Her candid
address gave the volunteers a new and deeper insight into
the problems and difficulties of those who are both blind
and elderly.

She is alone in the world now, for her only daughter lives
in America. Recently, when unable to sleep she tried to
make a cup of tea in the middle of the night. She knocked
over a kettle of boiling water and scalded herself. Yet her
cheerfulness is a tonic, and that is why she always has a
waiting list of volunteers who wish to help her.

Another blind lady was very different. For her nothing
in life was ever quite right. Every visit began with a long
recital of woes. Whenever she telephoned me, which was
often, she began with the words, "I'm feeling much worse
today." I knew immediately who it was although she rarely
gave her name.

It was extremely difficult to persuade her that volunteers
were not able to stay overnight. No visit was ever long
enough to suit her. She even found it hard to understand
why a volunteer could not be supplied to accompany her on
a flight to Ireland during term-time. She had quite irra-
tional fears about her central heating system which she
expected to blow up at any time. This puzzled the volunteers who were told they must prevent it at all costs, but at
last they realised that her fears were groundless and due to
excessive nervousness. The weather never suited her either.
Although she was comfortably off she felt that life had
been very unkind to her. It was difficult to be sympathetic.
Yet her needs were real. She wanted reassurance and company. Her eccentricities were a challenge. One American
volunteer rose to it admirably. After having listened in

astonishment to her catalogue of complaints, he inter rupted,

"Say, Miss A., why do you complain so much?"

She was so stunned by this blunt question that for a time at least she stopped grumbling. She made many requests for this boy to be sent to her afterwards. He had gained her respect and confidence.

It may be felt that the blind are well looked after. Blindness receives universal sympathy. It is true that associations for the blind and other voluntary organisations do much to help them. All the same, there are many services the young can give which they often do not receive from anyone else.

Deafness is less obvious, and public sympathy for it is not so easily aroused. We were once addressed by a deaf lady who, after years of blindness, had regained her sight only to lose her hearing shortly afterwards. She claimed that deafness was worse, for people made less allowance for it, and became easily irritated and impatient.

Few people know quite what to do for those who are also dumb. Their affliction can condemn them to almost complete isolation from society.

Youngsters have an important role to play in arousing greater sympathy and concern. They can in many practical ways bring aid and new interests, as well as friendship and compassion, to those who are afflicted.

Chapter 7

HELPING THE HANDICAPPED

S HE HAD BEEN A GAY and active girl. At one time she led a
cub pack and scouting had been one of her main in-
erests. She used to play the accordion. Life was good; she
enjoyed it to the full. Then one day as she was coming home
from a dance she felt dizzy. Unable to walk straight or keep
her balance, she knew what it must be like to be drunk. But it
was much more serious than that. She had multiple sclerosis.

When we first met her she was already confined to a
wheelchair. She was gradually losing the use of her limbs,
yet her spirit was unconquered. She even held fast to a
cheerful though unreal optimism that a cure for the disease
was just about to be discovered. Since then she has grown
much worse, and has become blind. We have seen hope die
within her. Although she is as brave as ever there is now an
unspoken acceptance of the inevitable.

It was for her as much as anyone that the Physically
Handicapped Youth Club was originally formed. There has
been for some years a flourishing adult Society for the
Physically Handicapped in the area, but it was felt that the
young people needed a club of their own. In particular they
wanted the opportunity to mix freely with other young
people. So in 1964 a club was formed *with* them, not *for*
them. The Birmingham Young Volunteers' Trust has now
begun this work on a large scale and hopes to extend it.
Here the club is called the PHAB Club, the initials stand-

ing for Physically Handicapped and Able-bodied. Thus the essential principle of such clubs is made clear.

The girl in charge of physically handicapped youth work for the Solihull Young Volunteers is herself handicapped. Not only does she work hard as the Club Secretary, but she also helps spastic children in a special school. Her lively personality and her courage in overcoming her own handicap make her an inspiration to those she helps.

One of the boys we send to help the spastic children learn to swim is himself a polio victim. He can walk only with difficulty, but he is a splendid swimmer. The way he has mastered his disability is an example to the handicapped children. It would be hard to imagine anyone more suitable to help them. He has also done good work visiting and serving old people.

Both these handicapped volunteers are firm proof of the importance of letting physically handicapped youngsters serve with the others. They have an equally valuable part to play and always set a courageous example.

The club holds its meetings in the Methodist church hall, and has a varied programme. We try to make sure that the activities are not too static. Mobility is one thing that handicapped young people want, and it is our aim to provide it. Indoor programmes include party games and Beetle Drives. Conjuring, monologues, concerts and "Juke Box Jury" evenings have proved successful. Folk singing is popular, especially when everyone is able to join in. Film shows and coloured slides on winter evenings help to remind us of summer holidays and outdoor events. Whatever the programme, there is always time set aside for refreshments and a chat.

We do not forget the needs of others. Coffee evenings and Bring-and-Buy Sales are held to raise money for such charities as cancer relief, the Mission to Lepers and an outing for patients of a local mental hospital. We also entered a float in the town's carnival procession. All Club members play a full part in organising and running these activities.

The summer months give plenty of scope for outings. These have included trips to Warwick, Stratford-upon-Avon and Kenilworth Castle. On one occasion we visited Coventry Cathedral. Outings to the theatre have been appreciated. One unfortunate experience, however, taught us the importance of making sure of the quality of the show beforehand. Such visits must be entertaining.

Young volunteers help at the meetings and outings of the adult group, too. Two boys run a useful library trolley service, while others serve the refreshments. It enables them to get to know better the people visited during the week. On the summer outings sturdy volunteers push the handicapped in their wheelchairs round the grounds of historic homes. They also assist with the loading and un-loading of the chairs.

By far the biggest outing is the Christmas shopping expedition organised by the Birmingham Young Volunteers' Trust. Such outings have been carried out in many different parts of the country. Although we cannot claim to have been first in the field with this service it is doubtful if it has yet been done anywhere on a more massive scale. Almost four hundred handicapped and elderly people were taken last Christmas to the Bull Ring Shopping area in the city centre, where a similar number of volunteers awaited them.

The very large Woolworth's store was specially opened, the assistants having voluntarily given up their free half-day. The boys and girls rushed forward to assist handicapped people from coaches, ambulances and private cars. They were soon wheeled or helped into the gaily decorated store which they had entirely to themselves. The whole complex venture, involving careful synchronisation of almost a thousand volunteers, transporters, and elderly and handicapped people was carried out with precision. There were moments of difficulty when it seemed as though we should run out of wheelchairs, or even volunteers. At one such moment a long-haired youth in tight blue jeans and a check shirt sauntered towards me, dragging a docile young lady behind him.

"Wot's gooin' on 'ere, then?" he asked. I explained, and then, almost as an afterthought, added, "Like to help?"

"Wot us?" he said, incredulously. His girl friend looked positively alarmed, and began to tug at his arm. I thrust one of the few remaining wheelchairs into his hands. With words of encouragement I urged him towards the latest coachload of old people. The last I saw of them both was when they were wheeling an extremely grateful handicapped lady, in a slightly embarrassed, but willing manner round the first floor.

A blind lady was helped round the store by girls from a secondary modern school in one of the toughest parts of Birmingham. "You know," she said to me afterwards, "I couldn't have been given two kinder or more thoughtful girls."

One lady in a wheelchair had not been inside a shop for more than forty years. It was her birthday. The volunteers made it one of the happiest she could remember. In addition she had the pleasure of seeing a large smiling photograph of herself in the evening edition of a Birmingham newspaper.

Despite the great numbers, all were successfully coped with. The administration of this huge enterprise was car-

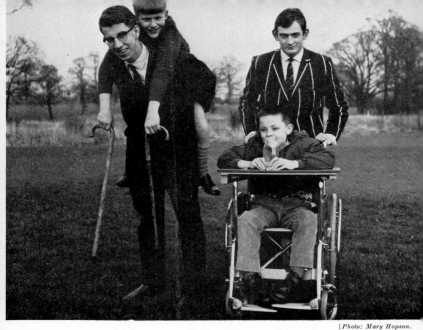

Helping the handicapped homeward bound.

[Photo: *Mary Hopson*.

[Photo: *Mary Hopson*.

Merryl Cross, herself handicapped, caring for children in a special school.

Young eyes for old.

A young volunteer opening a new interest for the mentally handicapped.

ried out entirely by Jane Markham and her assistant, Angela, both under twenty at the time.

We once received a request from the Welfare Officer to send a volunteer to teach a crippled lady how to use her new wheelchair. The boy who went soon gave her the confidence she needed. He sat in it himself and, turning the wheels with great dexterity, moved it this way and that with apparent ease. He showed her how to negotiate the narrowness of her hall, and the awkward angles of the doorways. They were soon firm friends. We then discovered that she was very lonely, and living in most depressing conditions. The grime on the walls and ceiling of her large downstairs bed-sitting room cast a gloom. A faded door-plate told us that she had once been a piano teacher. We soon found her a volunteer who was also a pianist, and this delighted her.

Then a team of decorators set about her room, and in a few days it was clean and bright. As she spent many hours alone in bed we approached a volunteer who specialised in radio and television repairs. He obtained an old TV set and made it work for her as efficiently as one of last year's models. He installed it with a bedside remote-control switch. A sound radio was also provided, and the volunteers met the cost of the licence. She is now visited several times a week by boys and girls.

Unfortunately, as she had an old dog which could not get out of the house, an unpleasant clearing up job had to begin each visit. When the dog died the volunteers persuaded her, with difficulty, not to have another.

I have called to see her myself many times since we began helping her three years ago. I am constantly amazed that the volunteers tolerate such unsavoury conditions with such fortitude. From time to time anxious adults ask me if

c

I know what the youngsters are having to put up with, the implication being that too much is expected of them. My reply is always the same. I know. I, too, am amazed at what young people are prepared to endure. Yet, whenever I suggest that they might like a change they are most indignant.

"What, give up?" they say, surrounded by a chaos worse than the one they cleared last time. Their pained looks of astonishment quell any further suggestion of surrender. Since I know that they have transformed the old lady's life, I step out again into the fresh air, thankful that teen-agers today have the guts to keep at an unpleasant job. The truth is that no adult organisation would take over their work if they deserted her.

It is this reliability and persistence which are so refreshing, and to some people so surprising, about young people. When we began it was quite apparent that many adults thought it would not last. Organisation is necessary, of course, but given that, young people are at least as reliable as adults, often more so.

We have a team of volunteers detailed to go every day of the week to one address. They go each morning at 7.30 and each evening at 9. Their sole responsibility is to help a lady lift her handicapped husband out of and into bed. Of course, they find ways of doing more than that, but this is why they are sent. The woman has a hard struggle to care for a man made helpless by multiple sclerosis.

"He's getting worse," she said to me as I left after a recent visit. "If it were not for the boys I could not manage any more."

The companionship and help of these boys and girls mean so much that absolute reliability is essential. The volunteers show that they have it in abundance.

It would be wrong to conclude any account of our work

with physically handicapped people without introducing Bill. He is a great favourite. As a young adult he is a regular member of the club. His head is large compared to his small body, and he finds great difficulty in walking. Without help he can just get along by using two sticks. If we hold him up firmly under one arm, he needs only one stick. Bill is convinced that he is the traffic controller for the whole of the Solihull district, and his influence extends far beyond. He can be seen about the town any day on his tricycle, which he manages well. He wears a large peaked cap and badges. There is little that Bill does not know about traffic conditions, car numbers and bus routine. On these he is a mine of information. The bus crews know him well, and he often chats to them as he does to the policemen on duty. He brings his large stiff-covered book to the club. This contains all his notes in very big printing. Woe betide any other club member who dares to take notes during the evening! It is the one thing which upsets his normally cheerful manner. He suspects them of trying to take over his job which includes the general reporting of club events.

One of Bill's most endearing characteristics is his strong sense of humour and fun. If we tell him a joke he is very responsive and is sure to have a witty reply. Without him the club would be lacking someone of real individuality and friendliness.

It is not possible in this book to portray each of the physically handicapped members of the club, though there is much of character and courage to tell of them all. Mention must be made, however, of one more, Susan. She is tiny. Barely three feet tall, though now adult, she faces life with a considerable disadvantage. Yet she does not allow this to prevent her playing the fullest part. She does much of the secretarial work, and types club correspondence. She organises whist drives and dances to help club funds, and in a number of other ways makes a very full contribution to its development. From its earliest days the club has owed much to her energy and interest.

Recently we suggested having a fancy dress party to start the new club season in the autumn. It was greeted with enthusiasm. Susan smiled.

"Whenever there's a fancy dress party," she said, wryly, "I get asked to play the part of one of Snow White's dwarfs. I leave you to guess which one." It turned out to be Dopey. We all laughed. It was typical of her humour, and of the club spirit generally.

The able-bodied members who inspired it would be the first to acknowledge the debt owed to their handicapped friends. Without them and the encouragement and guidance of members of the adult Society for the Handicapped, the work could not have grown so successfully.

The volunteers themselves learn a great deal from the handicapped people they serve. They see endurance and courage that they might otherwise never have met. The devotion of husbands and wives, whose partners have been made helpless, and of parents for their handicapped children, shows them the best in human love. The resolution with which people face the most appalling handicaps, and their skill in mastering them, compel the greatest admiration. Two of the people the boys visit have had both legs amputated. Another lady is not only confined to her wheelchair but also has her fingers so bent and crippled that they are useless. Yet all three, like so many others, show real strength of character. They harbour no resentment that life has been so hard. The volunteers find serving them a humbling experience.

Chapter 8

WORK WITH THE ELDERLY

'I'M IN ME EIGHTY-THIRD," she says triumphantly, whenever I visit her. Then she smiles with genuine delight. I must check with the Birthday secretary one day. She seems to have been in her "eighty-third" for a long time.

She is the tiniest old lady we visit, and she lives in the tiniest house. It is a two-roomed Elizabethan cottage. The roof beams are so low that even a man of medium height has to lower his head. The rooms are so small and narrow that it is almost possible to touch opposite walls at the same time. The boys love visiting her. They chop her firewood, dig her garden, clip her hedges and trim the paths. Above all they chat to her and take a real interest in her. She is always very pleased to see them.

An old man was heartbroken as his wife had died only a month previously, and for him life would never again be the same. The walls and ceilings of his room were blackened, but he would not let us re-decorate them. He did not want anything changed, but he was glad to receive volunteers. Gradually they overcame his intense loneliness, and although at first he had little to say to them he opened up considerably as the weeks passed by. They mended his electric fire, repaired his windows, tidied his garden and were soon indispensable to him.

Some of the more dramatic of our services to old people have already been considered quite fully, but visiting and serving them does not always present such difficult problems. Even so help is needed just the same. Old age is a handicap as we all realise each time we feel too old to undertake a particularly vigorous activity. It is a problem which our society is having to face on an alarmingly increasing scale. As people live longer so the numbers needing care and help grow. In Birmingham alone the size of the problem threatens to overwhelm existing voluntary and statutory organisations unless many more volunteers are forthcoming. Only the young have a sufficient reservoir of energy and drive from which further help can be drawn.

In our neighbourhood several hundred old people are now visited by young volunteers each week. Much is being done in their homes and gardens which would otherwise be wholly neglected. We have teams serving on large housing estates where the friendly chugging of their rotary mower is a welcome sound. Others visit individual homes where they do housework and odd jobs, handle minor repairs and fit draught excluders.

Gardens always absorb a great deal of labour during the season. Sometimes volunteers have a real wilderness to conquer, but mechanical hedge cutters and the rotary mower help us to cover more gardens than would otherwise be possible. Often on a big estate one house is used as a base. At the end of the afternoon the boys are glad to return there for a welcome cup of tea.

The visit itself is at least as valuable as the work done. It certainly means as much to the very old. Two years ago volunteers found an old lady who, after a fall, had dragged herself into bed and had lain there unvisited by anyone for three days. When they arrived she did not want to be bothered, but they soon cheered her up and had her out of bed sharing tea with them before the visit was over. She has since died, but towards the end the boys and girls were her only companions.

Although the story of young volunteers doing this work is overwhelmingly successful, mistakes are sometimes made. Equally, some volunteers work harder and achieve more than others. No one who has any knowledge of young people or an understanding of the differences that exist in personality and character, would expect otherwise. There are occasions when their well-meaning efforts are defeated by the weather. A hundred volunteers sent out to serve on a pouring wet afternoon will not achieve much unless the old people have the initiative and thoughtfulness to invite them to do something inside. Fortunately, they usually do.

When our group first started its small team of boys determined to serve whatever the weather. They did not wish to earn the reputation of fair-weather volunteers. They persevered in removing weeds from an old lady's garden despite a steady downpour. Unfortunately, the only access to her back garden was through the house. Mud squelched everywhere. She was further annoyed when she learned later that some of her favourite plants had been mistaken for weeds and removed. Their reputation would have suffered less had they been prepared to call it a day, and waited for a more suitable occasion. I am afraid I did not advise them well.

Another time volunteers worked industriously painting the ceiling of a large room, a back-aching job at the best of times. When late at night they left their work it was with some pride that they surveyed the clean, white expanse of ceiling which previously had been a dingy brown. Their distress on returning next morning to find the plastic emulsion dangling in long strips from the ceiling was understandable. It had peeled during the night, presumably because the base had been insufficiently prepared. It meant two extra days' labour, scraping the rest off again and repainting the entire surface with three coats.

We were very definitely learners in those days, but now we always try to have at least one experienced volunteer on the job. The Decorating secretary builds up his teams with great care, and supervises most of the work himself. A thorough list of decorating hints has been drawn up and copies are issued to volunteers starting this service for the first time. Even this may not cover every eventuality. Jane Markham once almost forgot to allow for the moon. She had been asked by a Health Visitor to decorate an old man's flat. She had been warned that he was eccentric, but harmless, except when there was a full moon. On these occasions he had been known to attack the lady on the floor above him. She discovered, to her dismay, that the week end she had arranged for volunteers to decorate, coincided with such a period. So, rather than take any risks, she postponed the project, the first time that young volunteers have been restrained by a phase of the moon.

Generally the old folk are most grateful, and their evident pleasure is reward enough, but on one occasion the boys were disappointed. They had spent several days decorating with great thoroughness the hall, landing and one bedroom of an old lady's home. When they asked her if she was satisfied she ran her finger along the top of the wardrobe and said, "Look, you've left some dust here." Since the job was one of the best they had done I greatly admired their self-control. Fortunately, she was not so ungrateful as she first appeared. Later, she told me how well she thought they had done. I passed her message on to the boys but wished she had been less critical at the time.

Sometimes we have jealous neighbour trouble. Boys painting the outside of one home were once embarrassed by envious neighbours who complained that the lady who lived there did not deserve their help. As the job had been passed on to us by the Welfare Officer we ignored their complaints. The work was duly finished. It had certainly been necessary. We would, of course, have been pleased to have painted the neighbours' houses, too, had they needed painting and our funds been sufficient. But the *real* need had to be there, not resentment.

Tape-recorded entertainment has proved very popular with both the volunteers and the elderly people whom they visit. This is a development of the service we first began for the blind. Now it is highly organised by Kenneth, the boy in charge of entertainments. The range of possible recordings is considerable. Music, stories, folk singing and pantomime excerpts have all been brought to the bedsides of elderly and handicapped people.

Regular film shows and musical programmes are also arranged by him in the Church hall. Transporting almost a hundred old people from private homes on these evenings is no mean feat of organisation. It could not be done without the willing co-operation of church members and other adults. Large numbers of volunteers wait on their elderly guests during the intervals and serve them with cups of tea, sandwiches and cakes. On one such evening a lively team of young Jewish volunteers presented a most attractive display of Israeli folk dancing.

Coach trips to city cinemas and theatres take place periodically. Within a few months volunteers have accompanied no fewer than two hundred elderly people on these outings. This quiet, shy organiser, Kenneth, who at school attracted no particular attention on the games field or in the classroom, has shown himself to be a first-class administrator.

The Birmingham Young Volunteers' Trust has helped to form a club for old people which meets in the new coffee bar club-room of the Association of Youth Clubs near the city centre. Every Friday afternoon boys and girls from King Edward's High Schools help the welfare organiser to run it, and occasionally Solihull School boys are able to provide musical entertainment. The club is now a great success and new friendships are being formed all the time.

An old lady set off for the club one day. She was over eighty but as she insisted on walking no transport was sent for her. Her balance was not good, however, and half-finished repairs made the path rough. She slipped and fell on her face, cutting and bruising it badly.

"Please help me," she called to a woman passing by. "I can't get up."

"Get up yourself," replied the woman callously, and left her.

Some while later the old lady staggered into the club-room, her face streaming with blood. The young volunteers and welfare organiser, who had been wondering why she was late, were horrified. Fortunately, one of the boys had borrowed his father's car. With a girl volunteer he took her to hospital where she had to have several stitches in her badly gashed nose. Afterwards they took her home, got into touch with her relations and did all they could to see that she was as comfortable as possible before they left her.

Recently two of our boys were faced with another serious situation. The old lady they were visiting had a stroke. They looked after her with great presence of mind, and called her doctor immediately. The Mayor happened to be visiting the home next door at the time, inspecting some volunteers decorating a hall and kitchen. He came in to hold the lady's hand and comfort her. Although she died from another stroke shortly afterwards the boys had been able to give her practical and much-appreciated aid. Within a fortnight the same two boys were helping a handicapped man when he had an internal haemorrhage. They were able to be a real help to the man and his wife.

When volunteers are undertaking visiting for the first time they need guidance. We try to provide it through briefing sessions and occasional talks arranged on different aspects of the work. A list of tips for volunteers has been compiled, and is given to new recruits. See Appendix II. It contains useful advice on how to make the first approaches, and the importance of reliability and thoroughness. The volunteer is also given a letter of introduction signed by the General Secretary. This reassures the old person that he is a genuine member of the group. We stress the importance of appearance and courtesy, for these are valuable in gaining confidence.

Occasionally there are difficulties. Some old people are not very easy to get on with, as their own relations freely admit, and others become very confused about little things. One old lady was convinced that her relatives and some adult voluntary workers were robbing her of gold watches that no-one had ever known her to possess. Fortunately, she did not accuse the youngsters, but once another old lady did. She had lost a plastic cup and saucer which she treasured. During the rather lengthy period of time in which the articles must have disappeared, the volunteers had spent part of an afternoon alone in the house, tidying up at her request. She could think of no-one else who could have taken them, though this somewhat vague accusation

was as far as she would go. We conducted the most searching enquiries, but the mystery remained unsolved. I found
it impossible to believe that the boys were even interested
in these cheap articles, and there was no proof against
them. It was, however, an unfortunate experience, and we
now advise volunteers not to remain in people's homes on
their own, even at the owner's request, unless there are
exceptional circumstances. There must always be trust between old folk and young visitors, of course, but risks
should be minimised. Where an organisation involves
several hundred volunteers visiting hundreds of homes it is
surprising that misunderstandings are so few.

We try to remember old people on their birthdays and at
Christmas time. Gifts and cards are taken to them and
special collections for this purpose are made in the schools.
Boys of Solihull Lower School made Christmas gifts for the
elderly a main theme of their Carol Service, and over two
hundred presents were brought.

A third form also compiled a large Christmas magazine
entitled *The Senior Citizen*. A boy's father printed six
hundred copies for distribution to old-age pensioners in the
area. It included poems, short stories, jokes, riddles and
articles on travel and many other interests. One boy wrote
an account of two years he had spent in the Fiji Islands.

The boys who wrote and edited the magazine were only
eleven years old. They were very thrilled to be helping the
Young Volunteers. They took copies themselves to patients
in the hospital geriatric wards, and others were handed out
at the Christmas party of the adult Physically Handicapped Society.

One of our big projects is the delivery of free coal to old-
age pensioners in the poorer districts of the city. Often they
find the cost of fuel so prohibitive that they dare not light

fires even in the coldest weather until the evening. During the day many of them sit huddled in their overcoats.

We advertise in our local newspaper asking for surplus coal. There are many homes in the area which have transferred to central heating, and the owners are usually pleased to have their coal-sheds emptied. Boys shovel the coal into bags, borrow a van or lorry, load it and accompany it into Birmingham where they deliver to addresses supplied by a welfare organiser. The old people are touchingly grateful and invite them in for tea. One old lady was so overcome that she wept with joy when the boys arrived with several bags of coal.

Serving and visiting the elderly is the largest part of our voluntary work. Their needs are so obvious and in many instances so simple to meet, yet without the youngsters they would often *not* be met. Companionship is undoubtedly what the elderly want most. The company of a young person for as little as an hour a week can make all the difference to them. Loneliness is their greatest fear and handicap, and it can be so easily banished. It is most gratifying to see the attitudes of old people towards the youngsters change as they get to know them and to appreciate their desire to help.

"They never used to do this sort of thing in my day," said one old man, shaking his head sadly.

In his voice I sensed not just a note of regret but a warm respect for the youngsters of the present generation.

Chapter 9

HOSPITALS AND HOMES

W E WERE SURROUNDED by them the moment we went
inside. They clapped us on the shoulders and
grinned. Some shouted greetings; others shook us warmly
by the hand. One pressed us to accept sticky and rather
grubby sweets. If we had refused he would undoubtedly
have been offended. Another made frequent and persistent
offers to wash my car. They were male patients of a mental
hospital.

Not for us the initial unresponsive reception that had
been reported from another mental hospital. Perhaps the
smaller size of the community led to a more friendly atmosphere, or perhaps the management was more enlightened.
Certainly, within the limitations of their budget, everything seemed to have been done to make the place as
homely as possible. Large dormitories were split into
smaller units and the lounges were pleasantly furnished
and decorated. The large Victorian institutional building
did not lend itself readily to modern adaptations, but we
were conscious of the effort made.

The chief male nurse and his deputy seemed as pleased
to see us as the patients were, and they welcomed any
opportunity to break down the barriers of ignorance and
prejudice which so often surround mental institutions. The
prospect of regular visits to the residents by young volun-

teers was one which pleased them very much and the boys received every co-operation they could wish for.

Our experiences in this hospital have been happy ones. The work there is still at a comparatively early stage of development, and we hope to do more in the way of entertainment. We have, however, made very encouraging progress with an arts and crafts group. We are rather proud of this venture for it is unique in the history of the hospital, and must be a very unusual form of youth voluntary service. It has been inspired and developed by one of my colleagues, an art master at school. He takes with him two artistic sixth-form volunteers, and together they instruct and encourage patients to develop self-expression and skill in drawing, painting and clay modelling. The therapeutic value is considerable.

"I don't mind telling you, this has shattered us," the chief male nurse said, as he showed me the paintings the men had done. It was their ability to concentrate for two hours or more at a time that surprised him most. Though much of the work is not very different in quality from that of five-year-old children, some have revealed unexpected talent. It should be remembered that these men cannot read, write or count. The subjects chosen have to be simple and direct, but the men have shown real feeling for colour and form. Their clay models of birds and animals have also attracted attention. Some of the work has been displayed to visiting parties and it is hoped in time to produce sufficient of a high enough standard to justify a small exhibition.

On Saturday afternoons volunteers take patients into the surrounding district. One of the favourite walks is to the local railway station where the men love to watch the trains. Their pleasures are often very simple. One outing was no more than a trip at night-time through the centre of the city when the streets were decorated for Christmas. The cries of delight and wonder left the organisers in no doubt about its success.

As young volunteers work with mentally handicapped people and come to realise how affectionate and good natured most of them are they may do much to create a new climate of opinion. Some mental hospitals have Open Days when volunteers can bring in their own friends and relatives to meet the patients they have been helping. Our art group played a valuable part on the last such occasion.

Work in general hospitals presents young people with many different kinds of opportunity and their help is usually welcomed by the nursing staff. The patients in geriatric wards are often in special need, for many of them seldom, if ever, receive visits from friends.

The social conscience of one volunteer was deeply stirred by the needs he saw. When he realised that many of the old men in the geriatric ward of Solihull Hospital had not been out for several years, he burst impetuously into matron's office. She was surprised by his request to be allowed to organise a ride for them in a special mini-bus, but his persuasiveness won her over and, permission granted, he was quickly on the telephone to me to ask me to act as driver.

"Sir," he said, resolutely, "we've just got to get them out! Some of them haven't been out of that place for ten years!"

I always recognise marching orders when I receive them from young people, and within a day or two I found myself driving a bus load of old men from the hospital through the lovely Warwickshire country roads to Stratford-upon-Avon.

The boy who had contacted me on the telephone sat at the back with the patients, chatting and looking after them. He pointed out the many changes that had taken place in their town. At Henley-in-Arden we stopped to buy some of the famous Henley ice-cream. Later we watched the pleasure boating on the Avon. It was a day none of us will ever forget.

We kept up our association with them, and girls now visit the old ladies. They help to feed and entertain them. It is hard going at times, for these very old people are often sleepy and not very responsive. When the weather is fine they are taken to the shops in wheelchairs. One patient was brought by his volunteers to the school chapel. There he was astonished to be greeted by the Chaplain, the Head-master and the Mayor. It was the beginning of the Mayor's tour of youth voluntary service in the borough.

A comparatively recent service to the hospital has been started to help friends and relatives visiting patients. A new reception office is manned by volunteers every evening at visiting times. Their job is to answer queries and direct people to the right wards. The volunteers are working a shift system, spending half their two-hourly period of duty in the office and a half on the wards.

Wards in six city hospitals have been adopted by volunteers from different schools. They assist at meal times, change the beds, and do other services helpful to both staff and patients. In the accidents and burns unit they prepare dressings. We also give after-hospital care in co-operation with the Health Department geriatric visitors. This includes the important tasks of cleaning and preparing homes for the return of patients, and sometimes involves redecoration.

One progressive school, the Harold Malley School for Boys, allows teams of volunteers to serve for a continuous three-week summer period after G.C.E. examinations have

finished. They are able to give considerable help in a
variety of ways in the wards, the administrative block, and
the X-ray department of the hospital.

Sometimes we have to meet unusual requests. Once an
urgent plea was made for a volunteer who could write
letters in Russian for a cancer patient. The General Secretary was able to find one at a moment's notice. It is partly
the swiftness with which youngsters can meet an unexpected situation that makes their help so valuable.

Visiting in a cancer home may seem to some adults a
grim task for the young. One boy reported that at least
seven of the patients he had been visiting had died during
the previous fortnight. But the preparedness of young
people to face reality, however unpleasant, is one of their
strong virtues. They do not wish to be shielded from
suffering and death, and we make sure that they are
fully briefed on what to expect, are wholly willing to
undertake the service, and mature enough to cope with the
emotional stress involved. With these precautions we send
our volunteers to visit serious cases, and always their contribution is welcomed. For most of the patients these
youngsters provide some of the last acts of kindness and
service they will ever know.

Work in homes for old people is not without its amusing
side. Certainly any matron unfortunate enough to be without a sense of humour must be at a serious disadvantage.
Life with the old is not by any means all sadness and
sympathy. One boy discovered this for himself when he
went shopping for some old people. He brought back a bag
of sticky buns for one lady but they were not the kind she
wanted, and in her wrath and indignation she hurled them
at him! He was later able to placate her, but the incident
was a lesson. In future he remembered to write detailed

shopping lists before setting off. Volunteers who do the shopping take a careful note of the amounts of money given, the particular brands of articles required, and shops preferred. Wherever possible separate receipts are obtained from the shopkeepers. At least the prices are written down, and to avoid confusion the change is carefully counted as it is handed back. Regularity is most important, for the old folk have their shopping lists ready for the day when volunteers usually call, and these days are eagerly awaited.

Visits which have a definite purpose help new volunteers to overcome any initial shyness. Help at meal times is one of these. The more infirm need assisting to their tables. Serving the food helps youngsters to establish contact, which often develops into friendship.

So, too, with entertainments and hobbies. Volunteers read popular books in serial form; and others run whist drives and bingo sessions. A boy from Tudor Grange Grammar School has built up a splendid film service and takes film shows to all the Old People's Homes in turn.

These services are not always done without difficulty. Two volunteers were upset when the old people of the home they were visiting told them to turn off their tape-recording shortly after the entertainment had begun so that they could watch television. The matron was embarrassed and the secretary of the home later sent a letter of apology to the boy in charge. At least he appreciated that the young people had given up a whole evening to offer this entertainment and was dismayed at the discourtesy shown by the residents. On the other hand it revealed the importance of choosing times for such activities carefully to avoid clashing with other interests. The volunteers concerned are now taking their recordings to old people living alone, and their efforts are always welcomed.

Residents also share in specially arranged outings and shows. These are particularly popular because a change of environment is always a tonic.

An amusing incident occurred on one of these outings, though it was worrying at the time. Despite careful transport arrangements a matron lost one of her men residents after a visit to a Harvest Festival. From what was known of his former habits she deduced that he must have gone to a local public house. As he was a new resident and not very responsible she was particularly anxious about him. So we had to comb all the public houses in the district on a Sunday evening, trying in each to describe the missing man. The police were informed, and there was quite a stir; but he turned up in the end. It appeared that he had been returned to the home after the service, but before matron and the rest arrived he had slipped out again to visit a relative who lived nearby. As it was very late when he returned he was naturally not in matron's good books!

There are several different kinds of homes in our district, and opportunities to help vary, but active service by young volunteers is going on in them all. Much depends on the matron or warden, and here we have been most fortunate. Almost without exception they have proved both welcoming and imaginative in their use of young people. I can recall only one instance in which a matron has made it really difficult for us to establish contact with the residents. She always seemed to find reasons why the volunteers should not meet the old people and her excuses were very lame. Usually she said the residents were too tired or did not want to be bothered. Since then there has been a change of matron and the situation is very different. Now the youngsters are given a real welcome and the old folk love to see them. Residents are naturally very dependent upon their matron, though this is less true in homes established on the "Abbeyfield" pattern. In these the residents occupy bed-sitters, usually in a large converted house. They may have communal meals and share the lounges if they wish, or look after themselves almost entirely and receive visitors at any time. Should they fall ill there is someone to look after them.

Recently the local council established a large modern block of flats for elderly people on similar lines in the midst of a pleasantly developed estate. The warden happens to be the Divisional Welfare Officer for the Red Cross, and therefore has wide experience. Since she is also a good friend of the young volunteers, and has worked closely with us from the beginning, we have excellent opportunities here.

A most successful venture is the art and craftwork developed by some of our girls in one of the homes. The old ladies are particularly responsive and have done some good modelling and painting. The girls collect wool for knitting blankets. Attractive displays have been made of duce the best work. Lively competition is always a that in this field there are far wider possibilities. I should like to see friendly competitions developed between the homes to stimulate competitive interest. Perhaps volunteers could vie with each other to see which homes could pro- their papier mâché models and paintings. I am convinced stimulant.

With little to live for, old people have not much to do except sit and look at the walls or at television and anything which breaks monotony and boredom is a most welcome relief. It is well known that a little exercise each day is an important aid to well-being. Therapeutic treatment is widely accepted and its value is beyond dispute. Yet because of shortage of staff in hospital geriatric wards the pathetic decline of old people with nothing to occupy their minds and hands is very common, and obvious even to the casual visitor. The patients often become so drowsy that the nurses have to prod and shake them to gain their attention for a few minutes.

Creative occupation keeps minds and limbs supple. Just as it is better to go out shopping *with* an old person, rather than *for* them, so it is better to share other activities with them. Entertainment has its place, of course, but it is noticeable how much more folk singing means to them when they are given an opportunity to join in. They enjoy active participation. We had a good illustration of this at Christmas when a group of girls from Olton Court Convent School handed round sheets of carols to the nurses and patients of the hospital geriatric wards, and everyone joined in lustily.

The way in which the introduction of fresh interests and youthful enthusiasm has brought a new vitality to some of the homes we visit is most marked. Though voluntary service is not so urgently needed by them as it is by old people living alone, it still has a valuable part to play. Youngsters soon realise how constructive and worthwhile their services can be. Any disappointing experiences they have had are more than offset by their successes.

Chapter 10

HELPING CHILDREN

THEY WERE SO AFFECTIONATE that the occasion was a little embarrassing. One small boy seized my arm, pressed it to his face, and kissed it eagerly. For several minutes he clung to me almost desperately. He was a handicapped child about seven years old, and we were in our school tuck shop. This small treat had been arranged with the matron of a school for physically handicapped children. There were eight of them, selected because they were deprived of parental affection. As they were so young we had invited two volunteers to help us from the neighbouring High School for girls.

It was a great success. The fizzy drinks and cream buns were lingered over with relish. Then we gave them piggy-backs. The children loved it. They clamoured for more. We showed them round the school and grounds. Although it was commonplace to us they seemed very thrilled by it all. The Hawker Hunter aeroplane standing beside the C.C.F. Headquarters was a great attraction, and they asked to be lifted up so that they could clamber all over it. When the time came to return only the pleasure of another trip in the old school bus softened their disappointment. Although so simple, this was one of the most gratifying outings we have yet arranged for them.

Work with physically handicapped children is particularly rewarding because during childhood so much can be done to help them overcome their disabilities. This recognised fact was brought home forcibly to me by our own handicapped secretary, Merryl. When she was tiny she was liable to collapse when walking with her father, and she told me how he insisted that she got up and tried again until she walked properly although she had one leg only half the length of the other. In spite of her considerable disability her parents had decided since her birth to administer this strong treatment. She was made to face and overcome her handicap.

"We realised at once," her father told me, "that we could do one of two things. If we gave her pity she would grow to be sorry for herself. So we did the opposite and brought her up the hard way to make her rise above her handicap."

"I hated it at the time," said Merryl, "but I bless him for it now."

As well she might, for few non-handicapped girls are more athletic than Merryl. She runs, swims and plays games as actively as any, and has even been awarded her school gym colours. Tennis is one of her favourite sports and she is very good at it, despite her restricting caliper. Once when she was trying out a new appliance in the hospital grounds it collapsed beneath her. She had to hop on her one good leg all the way back to the hospital buildings and then along the corridors to the ward. Her parents attitude had undoubtedly helped her to face such situations with courage and resourcefulness.

Many handicapped children do not have the parental wisdom and understanding that she has had. But without sentiment, young volunteers can step in and help them to build the confidence and determination needed to adjust themselves to their disabilities. They may feel sorry for them but they must never show it, for pity is wholly out of place when dealing with handicapped children.

We once took sixty of them on a Christmas shopping expedition to the town's largest department store. They were accompanied round the Toy Fair by almost twice as many volunteers. We shall have to reduce the number of volunteers another year, but so many wanted to help that it was hard to refuse. The children were given ten shillings each to spend as they wished. This money had been raised by the combined efforts of the Physically Handicapped Youth Club and the young volunteers. The store had organised a magnificent treat, for some of its staff had given up their free half-day to help. Father Christmas was there, too, with a friendly word for each child. Before they went home he gave them all sweets and balloons. It was the most wonderful shopping spree they had ever known, for they had been treated as normal children.

In the summer months we take them out for coach rides into the countryside. Volunteers have taken some of them to the circus and to a city museum. Many of them regard it as a great treat just to be taken into someone's home. A colleague of mine took one child to his home for tea. It was quite an ordinary house but when he was taken into the living room for the first time the little boy's eyes opened very widely.

"Cor," he said, gazing round in disbelief, "it's a palace!"

Being able to share in normal family life means a great deal to a deprived child. Invitations to join in on special occasions can mean even more.

We once had a family camping holiday in the Welsh mountains with our neighbours. A small boy from Coventry, whose father had been sent to prison, came too. The happy way in which he entered into everything added to our own enjoyment. Although he came from a large family where money was scarce he was very generous. He was always anxious to share any small thing that was given to him. He had never seen the sea before. He was thrilled when we found an unbroken stretch of sand several miles long. His first visit to the seaside became, for us all, one of the most memorable moments of the holiday.

Girls are always especially good with children. Pupils from Tudor Grange Grammar School were helping the physically handicapped and deprived children in the locality long before the co-operative scheme of service was launched. They still serve in the Special School and Reception Centre in considerable numbers, though volunteers from many other school groups have now joined them. They take children into the local parks, to the swings and slides, and to feed the ducks. At night they help in the dormitories, remove the calipers of physically handicapped children and clean their shoes. They help the house-mothers to bath them and put them to bed. At meal times they take the trolley round and serve the food. They love the work.

The children always give them a tumultuous welcome, hanging eagerly on their arms and plying them with questions. To them the young volunteers are like big sisters or brothers, and their affection is very touching. No wonder we always have more volunteers for this work than we can use.

The boys develop hobbies and interests with them, both in the classroom and after school. Stamp collecting, chess, model railways, Meccano modelling and painting are a few of the indoor activities with which they help. Some volunteers teach the children how to swim, but under the supervision of a member of the staff. Others organise games of cricket and football. This may seem strange with physically handicapped children, but many are able to manage, including those who have to hobble about on sticks.

One of our favourite tasks is the entertainment of mentally handicapped children at their parties. They enjoy our "Pop" groups with all the drums and electric guitars. Their sense of rhythm is not different from that of normal youngsters. Oblivious of their handicap they dance with uninhibited delight, and their enjoyment is a pleasure to see.

Our young volunteers have now begun a baby-sitting service for parents of mentally handicapped children. We hope this will grow, for the parents often find it almost impossible to go out for an evening together.

In the city volunteers have established several nursery play groups for children of pre-school age. There are many from broken homes, or whose parents both go out to work, who urgently need this service. Help is being given by students from university or college, and we have appealed in a local newspaper for toys of all kinds, including tricycles, rocking horses and dolls' houses.

The Birmingham Young Volunteers have also established a most successful summer camp in co-operation with the city's Association of Youth Clubs. Children from deprived and broken homes have been selected to go to this by the Family Service Unit and other agencies. Last year over six hundred were taken to the camp in the grounds of Windmill House, the Association's fine residential conference centre in Worcestershire. Many of them stayed for a week at a time while others were collected daily by coach and taken to join in the camp's games and activities.

Volunteers willingly manned the camp throughout August, organising the programmes, providing meals and administrating. Children of many different races and colours mingled happily together. It was good to see them chasing each other across the camping field, or kicking a ball about on lush grass instead of on the desolate city sites of demolished buildings or in dingy slum streets. The project may have helped just a little towards alleviating the vast immigrant problems of the city, though these now loom so large that almost any effort short of a massive civic or national plan seems totally inadequate. As, however, debates continue on the educational and housing problems, voluntary bodies should give what help they can, and at once.

By the time the Lord Mayor and Lady Mayoress of Birmingham arrived to inspect the camp, continuous heavy rain had churned the ground into a sea of mud. But our distinguished visitors soon realised how much everyone was enjoying it. They were impressed by all that they saw. The spirits of the children in particular had not been dampened by the rain. It was adventure, and they enjoyed it.

Many of the campers had never seen a cow before. The actual process of milking caused the greatest astonishment. "But, Miss," exclaimed one dirty, pale-faced boy, incredulously, "milk's made in bottles!"

The children were so happy at camp that several turned up at the collection centres and begged to be allowed to return for a second week. The morning after the camp had finished and all the children had left for home, three forlorn and weary small boys suddenly appeared on the camp site.

"Where's Aunty Jane?" they anxiously asked those who were clearing up. "Aunty" Jane was duly fetched and the children begged to be allowed to stay. The eldest child was twelve, the others only two and three. They came from Sparkbrook near the centre of the city and had travelled all the way on their own, by bus as far as the city boundary and then on foot for the *last six miles*.

The volunteers gave them a good meal and played with them before taking them home. For these children home was little more than a roof over their heads. The windows and doors were missing and there were no beds. The whole family slept on the floor with trench coats as their only covering. Their mother was pregnant and has since given birth to twins. Such children are imprisoned by life's circumstances unless we can set them free.

Community Service Volunteers have also helped to meet the city's immigrant problems by teaching Pakistani children. They have not only taught them to speak and write simple English, but have also made real efforts to befriend them. One volunteer took some of the boys home with him to camp in the grounds of his public school in the south of England.

We sent five Solihull School boys as tent leaders to a camp for deprived children held in the Cotswolds. It was organised by Toc H at their beautifully situated centre, Dor Knap, near Broadway. It was a challenge, for the volunteers had some very tough boys in their care. Most of them were on probation. One had stolen a van and been chased at high speed down a motorway before he was caught by the police. Others had been in trouble for vandalism and truancy. Another was an outright bully; it was hard to protect the smaller boys from his aggressive behaviour.

"Wot you done, then?" one twelve-year-old boy asked his tent leader. He expected all camp members to be in trouble of some kind. The tent leader, who was only fourteen himself, made a non-committal reply, and changed the subject. The aim was that the volunteers should mix completely with the rest, and be accepted as belonging to them. Any emphasis of difference would have asked for trouble. It was not easy, but camping is always a great leveller.

Later I asked them what they thought about it.

"It was fantastic, sir," said one boy. "I wouldn't have missed it for anything."

"I was jolly tired at the end," said another. "We couldn't have stuck another week, but it taught us a lot."

What had it taught them? I wanted to know. So I pressed my question home, and asked one volunteer for his frank views. He hesitated for a moment, and then said firmly, "It taught me to handle Ingles, sir. I'd never met anyone like him before. I hadn't a clue what to do at first, but we got on quite well in the end."

"Ingles" was a mentally backward boy. To start with he had hurled various objects at his tent leader for no apparent reason. The other boys did not like him because he did no work, and would not co-operate. After some fairly good-humoured camp ragging he had become upset and run away. This meant a long chase across fields and over streams before he was caught. When his leader reached him he lay on the ground, half weeping, half laughing. His emotions were confused. He refused to move, partly because of sheer exhaustion.

"Cheer up, Ingles," said the leader, coaxingly. At first he would not respond, but eventually they returned to camp together. They both had learnt the difficult lesson of co-existence.

The holiday was an eventful one. It kept both the organisers and the volunteers on their toes. One day the boys left a farm gate open. It took a good twenty minutes to round up the flock of sheep that had escaped. On another occasion they sent a heavy cart careering down the hillside just for the fun of it. It crashed into one of the tents, ripping the canvas.

The axes were a problem, some of the campers brandishing them dangerously. Smoking was common among boys of all ages. On an outing to a nearby village several of them would have stolen postcards if the alert leaders had not prevented them.

One experiment was a great success. Each tent was allocated a deaf-and-dumb boy. By lip reading they followed intelligently the tent leaders' instructions. They helped their companions to learn their own manual sign language, and were popular because they worked so hard for their teams. The creation of a team spirit was the particular responsibility of the leaders, and by the end of the camp their success was obvious.

Our young volunteers also co-operate with Toc H at the Hampton Manor Home for mentally handicapped girls. This fine estate, which once belonged to Sir Robert Peel, founder of the British Police Force, was badly overgrown and needed restoring. Toc H adopted the project, and we sent teams of volunteers to help over a three-week period during July. Our girls are regular visitors to the home, but this was really a heavy labouring job for boys. In the summer we help at an annual fête nearby, running a sweet stall. The boys also do a brisk trade in pancakes and hot dogs. Although it is not usually our policy to become involved in fêtes we make this exception because it gives us a chance to work in close co-operation with the parents of the mentally handicapped girls.

The boys of the Lower School are also able to play a part, for they mainly provide the sweets. A competition is organised between various forms to see which can collect the most the week previously. This creates great enthusiasm among the small boys. When the day arrives they turn out in large numbers to buy back as many of the sweets as they can. They are delighted if any are sold to them at bargain prices. We always have more than enough, and any left unsold are given to the mentally handicapped children.

Similarly, older volunteers help in Packwood School for educationally sub-normal boys. They run scouting games and help with hobbies and other activities. Together with two resident Community Service Volunteers they recently ran a Duke of Edinburgh Award scheme. Several of the boys have already earned their bronze medals.

A very lively pantomime is staged annually in a church hall by the children of the local school for the physically handicapped. With the co-operation of the Red Cross, many old people are brought to see it. The youngsters handle all the stage management and lighting, and prepare and serve refreshments. It is undoubtedly one of the big days in the school year.

Work with children is always popular with volunteers. Though the problems of many of them are very serious their liveliness and capacity for enjoyment makes work with them most satisfying, yet some have problems for which we cannot yet hope to find an answer. I heard recently of two cases which are baffling even to professional child welfare workers. One concerns an eight-years-old boy whose father is an alcoholic. This child finds it very hard to accept that other adults are behaving normally, when they are so unlike his father. Another spastic boy is both incontinent and anti-social. He locks himself up in cupboards and refuses to speak to anyone.

It is not surprising that in such extreme cases the help of young volunteers is only cautiously accepted by profes-

[*Photo: Birmingham Post and Mail.*

Christmas shopping for the shut-ins.

[*Photo: Birmingham Post and Mail.*

No racial barriers at summer camp.

A helping hand.

[Photo: Lawrence

Warming to the task.

[Photo: Mary

sional workers. There are, however, such large areas of service among children in which their help is more than welcomed that these should be concentrated upon while leaving the serious cases to those qualified. Maybe there would be fewer serious cases. Their enthusiasm and reliability gain respect, and they are often able to win the confidence of children where adults cannot.

Few people realise how vast are these areas of need and opportunity for service among handicapped people. No less than ten per cent of all children have some form of abnormality. More than half a million of these have no special schools available, including well over ten thousand of the seriously handicapped. Mental Health Week in 1967 emphasised the critical need for more staff and teachers. The shortage is so grave that all the young volunteers we can find will be needed for years to come. Not that they can ever replace qualified staff but they can relieve the pressure and help in so many ways. An expert has recently calculated that by 1970 one eighth of all children will require special education. This means well over a million for whom there is little hope that the necessary forty to fifty thousand trained teachers will be forthcoming. It is essential that those who are trying to grapple with this seemingly overwhelming task are given every possible voluntary assistance. In this crisis of children in need, no less than with the elderly and the sick, only our teenage youngsters have the numbers, the energy and the enthusiasm to come to the rescue.

D

Chapter 11

UNFINISHED BUSINESS

Frances, one of our best volunteers, turned to me in exasperation.

"I don't want to know all the reasons why I am doing the things I am doing," she said. "I just want to get on and do them."

We were discussing the motives of young people doing community service. She had been a volunteer for years. Now she was the school secretary of one of our largest groups. Yet she was impatient with the argument about motives. She had my sympathy. Too prolonged introspection about the reasons behind life's socially worthwhile activities is not good. By the time we have worked out a philosophy of service which will satisfy everyone, many needs will have passed beyond the power of our solution. It is not sufficiently realised how urgent some of these are. Young people want action, not words.

Our council meetings illustrate this well. No nonsense here about undue formality. The general secretary controls the proceedings firmly but opinions and suggestions from the others are welcomed. They would be extremely bored with most adult committees, but they attend their own enthusiastically. Perhaps this is because their business is carried out so briskly and without digression.

The meetings are held in a church parlour. About thirty secretaries representing their groups, or special responsibilities, take part. This seems a large committee but it works well. Sometimes the most surprising items are introduced during routine business.

Kathleen, a quiet, but thoughtful young girl from Sharman's Cross High School, said she knew where we could obtain young budgerigars free. She thought perhaps some old people might appreciate their company. The others were amused by this unusual offer. In the three years the council had existed no one had ever thought of budgerigars before. They promised to ask their volunteers to make inquiries but thought the problem of providing cages might be difficult. No one knew that even as they were discussing it there was a letter in the post from an old lady whose budgerigar had just died. She had written to ask the young volunteers if they could possibly help her to get another one as she missed it so badly. The arm of coincidence is long indeed.

Although youngsters are impatient to get on with the work without asking too many questions, there will be moments when they pause fleetingly to consider their reasons. Their first answer is usually that they are responding to need. Sometimes the need takes an unexpected turn.

The boys had been sent to decorate an old couple's home. It was in a terrible state but the volunteers kept at it for several weeks. They worked hard, for they knew the old man had been gassed twice in the First World War and had been at Dunkirk in the second. He was beyond doing his own decorating and needed their help.

When the job was almost over I asked the headmaster to come and see their work. I knew it would encourage them. He willingly agreed. When we arrived the boy in charge took me aside.

"The old couple are in a bad way," he said quietly.

"Their dog died yesterday, after seventeen years with them. They're in tears, sir."

We knocked on the door and went into their small back room. He was right. They were very upset and close to tears.

"It's broke me 'eart," mumbled the old lady.

"I don't mind as I go meself, now," said her husband.

They felt their grief as if a child had died. They had no children of their own and the dog had meant everything to them. As we left I looked at the decorating. The boys had done well, for the job was almost finished. But with the old folk in that back room there was yet another job. It wasn't finished. It had only just begun.

This is the way with voluntary service by young people. We always have unfinished business. Even when we take on a task that looks straightforward and limited we find it leads to something else. We become involved, and inevitably there is always some unexpected need to meet.

Critics who describe voluntary service by young people as a salving of social conscience are wide of the mark. Certainly, my experience does not bear them out. It might be correct to speak of the awakening of social conscience in young people. I am sure this does happen as they delve into the needs and failings of society. I have known volunteers who began their service almost diffidently, become deeply concerned to right social wrongs which have made them indignant. But the guilt complex suggested by the phrase "salving conscience" belongs to the older generations, for it is they who are conscious of responsibility for the state of things as they are.

Cynics love to sneer at young volunteers who come from comfortable middle-class backgrounds, implying that their service includes an air of patronage. But this criticism is part of the British obsession with class. Everyone, it seems, has to be classified and labelled. When this has been done we are expected to pronounce some kind of judgment on their motives in all they do, or the unfairness of their being what they are. It is an unfortunate and socially divisive practice which can do only harm, and it is totally irrelevant to youth community service.

Some volunteers do come from comfortable homes, and from Public Schools or Grammar Schools. Others are from Secondary Modern Schools or Comprehensive Schools. Some live in prosperous suburbs, others in the heart of slumland. Who is bothered? Certainly the young people are not. They work together, without distinction or undue consciousness of difference. They belong to a rising generation which is intolerant of artificial barriers and division. They are faintly amused that the older generations are so often tilting at nineteenth-century windmills. They are not unaware that inequalities do exist, but they do not allow these to become an excuse for social paralysis. Nor do they make "value judgments" of their fellows on such a false basis.

Indeed, the motives of many adults who support youth voluntary service are sometimes more suspect than theirs. There are those who see the young volunteer as free labour to be exploited for jobs that a diligent and self-respecting society should have dealt with long ago. I am not in favour of young people being used for civic schemes that should be carried out by professional contractors. They ought not to be used like Chinese coolies to replace the bulldozers and excavators that an affluent society can well afford. This is not to say that I am against all large-scale projects involving manual labour, or arousing young people's concern for their environment. The Civic Trust has done splendid work fostering and organising such interests, but the dangers should be recognised and guarded against.

Another aspect to be considered cautiously is recruitment. Are genuinely voluntary principles being adhered to? Are large groups of youngsters being involved through their own enthusiasm, or just because certain adult leaders think it good for them? These are questions which need to be asked of every kind of community service, and we ought to be particularly careful when involving a large force of volunteers on manual labour. The temptation to make up numbers to meet the requirements of a big project is considerable. Head teachers, youth leaders, or task organisers can do much harm to young people's spirit of service by violating their elementary right to decide for themselves.

The real danger of this is clear from current discussions in certain educational quarters as to the advisability of including voluntary service in the school curriculum. To me the issue is simple. Voluntary service could be effectively programmed within a school's weekly routine, providing genuine alternatives are made available, no undue pressure brought to bear, and sufficient time allowed for the services to be effectively undertaken. This scheme has certain advantages, for it makes daylight work possible in the winter months, and enables joint projects to be carried through. But it is quite a different matter to make service compulsory, which, to my mind, destroys the very spirit and enthusiasm of it. Having heard the suggestion elsewhere, my own council of young volunteers showed emphatic disapproval.

"We would view it with horror," said Nigel, one of the senior boys, and the loud murmur of support for his remark left no doubt about the feelings of the others.

If a compulsory plan is tried on a universal scale the

whole development of youth voluntary service may well turn sour on us, and the adult world by its clumsy handling and misjudgment of the situation will have helped to stifle, if not destroy, the most promising idealistic movement among young people for half a century.

There is, of course, a tremendous opportunity looming with the approach of the raising of the school-leaving age to sixteen years in 1970. The revision of the schools' curriculum to make this extra year purposeful and worthwhile should take fully into consideration the opportunities of voluntary involvement of youngsters in schemes of civic and social responsibility. This would help to relate the final year to the realities of the world in which these youngsters will soon be earning their living.

When planning voluntary schemes it is important to select landscaping and constructional projects which have an immediate social significance readily understood by the youngsters. The more these bring them into direct touch with the people who are to benefit, the better. To plant a forest for posterity is one thing, and has its place, appreciated by those with a long-term vision of what they are doing. To create from a slum, what, by their efforts, has become a palace for an old couple living there, evokes a deeper response from most young people.

One of the safeguards is to give them a major say in the policy and planning of service, for they are quick to discern the genuine needs of society. An adult who regards them as units to be directed, instead of volunteers wanting to help, is unlikely to get very far.

Youngsters will always respond with deep concern to human deprivation or suffering, even when these arise from the neglect and failure of society. Their practical help for the homeless shows this as well as anything. For several days at Christmas young volunteers entertained, fed and cared for forty-nine homeless people at Windmill House. They arranged parties, and an outing to the pantomime. Father Christmas came with new toys for the children. It was a happier Christmas for the homeless than they had dared to hope for. While the State tolerates such problems young people will do what they can to help to alleviate them, providing they are given advice and opportunity.

To succeed in gaining the enthusiasm and loyalty of youngsters for such work an adult adviser must have a sense of social urgency himself. It is no good making a half-hearted approach. He must share their longing to play a positive role. He needs more than a touch of their own vitality and crusading spirit. There is always so much to be done. It does not matter where you live, the need round the corner can be as dramatic and intense as anywhere in the country. Here is one we have only recently discovered. The district is respectable and prosperous. There is a lane leading into the countryside, beginning with neat little rows of semi-detached bungalows and houses. Many possess a garage, and cars can be seen everywhere. Yet it is probably the grimmest situation in which I have ever placed volunteers. As I write this, boys are helping there, less than a mile away.

There is no sign of poverty except in one house. Here the jungle of bushes and hedges almost hides its disrepair, but not quite. Paint has long since abandoned the doors and window frames. Broken panes and boarded holes hint ominously at what might be the state inside. The tattered remains of an ancient curtain flap through a smashed attic window. The rooms inside are far worse than we imagined. The accumulation of filth and grime can hardly be described. A dead cat lay decomposing in one room for over two weeks before a Welfare Officer knew of it. Yet someone lives there. The physical shock of meeting her proved to be the worst moment of all.

We knocked hard on the door and held our breath. The doctor had warned me what to expect, and I had told the volunteers that what they were about to see would be unpleasant. Yet they had agreed to go through with it. It had not been the doctor's suggestion that they should help. I could not expect him to take the responsibility, though he assured me there was no risk to health.

After a long pause came a slow shuffle behind the door. A feeble rattle told us someone was trying to open it.

"Give it a push," she said.

We did. The warped wood jammed hard. Then it opened suddenly. One or two jerks, and there she was before us, leaning on an old rusted garden rake which served her as a stick. A faded brown fur coat, worn largely bald and shiny with age, was drawn round her. Her decrepit slippers were little better, but it was the face that held our attention. We could hardly bear to look. Yet to divert our eyes was too obvious and too unkind. If it was blood, not boredom, that the young volunteers wanted, then this was it. A skin complaint had bared her flesh down one side of her face. It engulfed one eye and spread across her left brow. It was raw, red and wholly revolting. Had we not been prepared we should have recoiled visibly. For a moment my stomach turned. The boys behind me must have felt the same. Then we remembered why we had come. As she looked at us with enquiring, distorted eyes we wondered how we should be received. We offered our help.

"You can't come inside," she said, as we peered past her at the desolation beyond. "There's nothing to do here since my husband died."

The futility of those words must have been obvious even to her. "You see, I haven't been very well lately," she said lamely.

There was no persuading her. We explained that the boys were good at decorating, but she countered by saying it was too cold. So we settled for an attack upon the outside wilderness. Then a neighbour appeared with an electric hedge-cutter for the boys to borrow. This was a great help. One boy measured the broken window frames. Only the week before he had done a good repairing job elsewhere.

We decided that it would be sensible to do the outside decorations first, for then only the volunteers would have cause to complain of the cold. So we put the suggestion to her. We were already beginning to win through.

"What are your favourite colours?" we asked persuasively as we saw her hesitate.

"Dark green and cream," she replied.

"Right then," we said, "we'll be back next Thursday, and the job will be done. There'll be a lot of us."

There were, too. We moved in on the job in strength. Over twenty boys worked there during the day and the dilapidated house was changed out of all recognition. We hope perhaps that her life will be, too. But this was only the beginning of what is likely to prove one of our most challenging tasks.

That we are discovering locally such grim situations several years after our voluntary service scheme began is a reminder of how much remains to be done, and it will not be finished in our lifetime.

Chapter 12

THE WAY AHEAD

WE BELONG to a careless generation. My last story and much else written in this book prove it. We have been weighed in the balance and found wanting; this by our own children, or teen-agers young enough to be our children. There are, of course, many people of whom this cannot fairly be said. They have shown a practical concern, and given a lifetime of service to others. Every age produces its social pioneers and its saints; the twentieth century is no exception, but this does not excuse our generation nor diminish our responsibility. We cannot contract out of society or pretend its failings are not our own. Most of us are in no position to do so.

Such judgment may seem harsh. How can we be accused of negligence, or lack of social concern? After all, we have created the Welfare State. How different things are today from the hardship and unemployment of the 'thirties! No one who has known the hunger and despair of those years, as I knew them in my early childhood, will ever forget. It cannot be denied that for the vast majority of our people life is better. We have forged a greater security than our fathers enjoyed. The gadgets in our homes and our overcrowded roads show a general luxury of life that former generations scarcely dared to dream of. The men who came back from the battlefields of Europe and the Far East at the end of the Second World War did so determined to build a better Britain. The politicians encouraged them in their hopes, and in many ways these seem to have been justified. In the light of our national progress since then, can it truthfully be said that they have failed?

I believe it can. We have all failed, and for a very simple reason. We have forgotten that man does not live by bread alone. Worse still, we have deluded ourselves into thinking that he lives on cake. Worst of all, we have spent our energy and our spirit striving to make sure that our particular slice is the biggest we can make it. We know in our hearts that the economic crises that have dogged us for twenty years are really crises of moral fibre and national character. It would take a bold and unperceptive student of our affairs to deny these assertions in face of the industrial, social and political history of the post-war era. He would certainly not receive a favourable hearing from the rising generation, for it is just here that their actions condemn us.

Not only those of idealistic, socially constructive youngsters either, but also those of the vandals and beatniks, the "junkies" and the sexual deviationists. They scorn our achievements, and older people are puzzled, indignant and angry. We have built them cities of chrome and they smash what they see. To some, youth seems monstrously ungrateful.

The more socially acceptable and conformist of our young people bring little comfort to our pride. They are far from uncritical of the society we have built for them. They are not prepared to stand by and accept our easy neglect of the real need. When we have sought to add a few shillings to the old-age pension, particularly around election time, they have seen that loneliness cannot be bought off with an allowance book. Where we have provided free pills for a neurotic society they have seen that companionship and genuine concern are a better medicine than can be obtained on National Health. Where we have left children scrambling aimlessly over derelict sites, they have created adventure playgrounds.

I do not decry the benefits brought by much post-war legislation, but they are not, and never can be enough. We have too often committed the error of supposing that they are. Nor do I exempt the Church entirely from criticism. Too often its decisions at local level reflect the spirit of the times more faithfully than the spirit of the Master. This may seem an inevitable outcome of the tensions which exist between its highest ideals and the secular influence of the society in which it bears witness. Yet such compromises leave it open to criticism on a number of counts, especially in this materialistic and cynical age.

I must, however, reiterate my experience that no organisation is better placed than the Church to introduce young people to opportunities of service. Of all the bodies concerned with the wellbeing of society, none is more so than the Church. Nowhere else is there so deep an understanding of what it is all about. Its own record in service to mankind during the past 2,000 years is unsurpassed. However much certain aspects of its history may be criticised, this should not be forgotten.

There are still millions of young people associated with the churches of all denominations, through Sunday worship, youth clubs and uniformed organisations. The decline of Sunday Schools which has taken place in recent years does not mean that the days of the Church's work with young people and children are numbered. Far from it. Church influence in this sphere remains enormous, and there are many signs that its ideas are being adjusted to meet new needs, with a deeper understanding of what is required. A real effort is being made by enlightened Christian leaders to present faith to the young in a way they can appreciate at their present stage of development. The new approaches are experiential, and in this, involvement in service to the community ought to play an important part. I hope it will not be neglected, for we must show our youngsters the real contrast between the caring love of Christ and the carelessness they so often see in the world round them.

This is sometimes revealed very clearly in the use of things that are treasured by society. The motor car is probably the most coveted family luxury of the century, yet we have made it the greatest killer. Just when distance presents no problem to the scattered family, in visiting and looking after Granny we have decided she would be far better off in a home.

Thousands of children are deprived of their parents when they need them most, because both are out at work all day. During school holidays they run the streets, uncared for and unloved in any way that has meaning.

Well over a third of the cases dealt with by the Birmingham Council of Social Service during 1966 resulted from "broken" homes. Very often it is the children who suffer most. For various reasons many of these innocent victims do not qualify for local government or state aid. Over thirty-five thousand people alone sought help from the Citizen's Advice Bureau in Birmingham in the same year. The magnitude of the national problem is immeasurable.

Yet young people everywhere are trying to bridge the gap. In many of our largest cities important co-operative schemes have developed in recent years with great success. There is no lack of support. Almost simultaneously with the birth of the Birmingham Young Volunteers' Trust in the late summer of 1965 came the Manchester Youth Community Service scheme. This was the result of the Lord Mayor's initiative at the beginning of his term of office in that year. Six standing committees were formed to deal with the main spheres of service. These were—old people, hospitals, handicapped people, children, special projects and landscaping.

Sheffield Youth Action is in many ways similar to the Birmingham movement. It, too, has developed through the dynamic and imaginative leadership of a young organiser, Peter Furniss, who has shown much administrative skill and tact in involving hundreds of young people in voluntary work. He made one most important breakthrough in hospital service by arranging for fifty girls from a secondary modern school to feed the patients regularly at mealtimes. A valuable factor in our own situation is the wholehearted co-operation of the Birmingham Association of Youth Clubs. It has not only lent the scheme its entire support from the outset but has also placed an office within its headquarters at the disposal of the Trust.

In the autumn of 1966 both Manchester and Bristol, with its "Service 9" youth voluntary service scheme, appointed full-time organisers, thus following in this respect the pattern of Birmingham and Sheffield. The Merseyside Young Volunteers, and youngsters of Cardiff, Coventry, York, Edinburgh and other large cities are all playing an active part in the remarkable, recent development of youth voluntary service.

One of the largest and most highly organised of all these groups is 1964 Task Force Limited which operates in several London boroughs with outstanding success. This is due partly to the drive and efficiency with which it is run and partly to the excellent financial support it has been able to attract. Its work is confined to the elderly, and here, certainly, there is no lack of service to be given.

In more rural situations the development of the Sevenoaks and Shrewsbury Schools' voluntary service units has been particularly noteworthy. Both bear some similarity to the Solihull scheme, with young people taking a leading role.

The "clearing house" principle in which services and volunteers are brought together through a central agency is common to all the large co-operative groups. Co-ordination is thus achieved.

It would be possible to add very many others to this list, equally interesting and worth mentioning, but these alone are sufficient to reveal how widespread the movement has become of recent years.

It is, of course, impossible to sustain large city schemes without financial support. The costs of administration, transport, and the organisation of camps for deprived children, or clubs for the physically handicapped, are considerable. With all the voluntary help in the world it still costs a lot of money to provide for, and feed, over six hundred children at a summer camp, and this is only one project.

In Solihull the generosity of the Local Council of Social Service has been a great help in meeting from its own slender resources the entire cost of decorating materials and the insurance of young volunteers. Solihull School Governors also meet the expenses of the school group, and the Local Education Authority gives grant-aid towards training conferences. For the rest, the efforts of the boys and girls in raising money through dances, jumble sales and school collections cover the costs of projects and equipment. But with big cities the problems are much greater. The vastness and concentration of city needs make it essential to employ full time organisers and secretarial assistants.

The work could never have begun in Birmingham without the generous support of private benefactors and trusts. Unless this is maintained and increased it cannot survive. It is hoped that city councils which make such full use of young people and reap the benefits of their labours will be imaginative and generous in recognising their moral and financial obligations. Youth deserves this help.

An enormous debt is owed throughout the country to the inspiration of the Community Service Volunteers. Of all the national organisations, none has done more to develop youth voluntary service, or to create the present favourable climate of opinion. Volunteers are recruited from schools, police cadets and industry, and sent, after consultation, all over the country. They undertake the widest variety of tasks, residing sometimes for several months, or a year, in their places of service. They are adopting increasingly catalytic roles, and have stimulated or begun many local schemes of voluntary service. The organisation is available for consultation and advice on all aspects of the work.

All these developments, exciting as they are, are rapidly being overtaken by events. For some time it has been evident that the Government is deeply interested in the recent upsurge of youth voluntary service. Those of us already in the field have been aware that some official action to support and encourage its growth has been imminent throughout 1967.

The negotiations taking place between the Minister for Youth and Sport and some national voluntary service organisations have now been extended to local authorities. Proposals arising from the findings of a working party led

E

by Mr. Gordon Bessey, Director of Education for Cumberland, have been fully studied by the Youth Service Development Council. As this book is being written the possibility of a national task force of Governmental backed Social Service units has been forecast in many leading newspapers.

In the present state of flux, if the Government is going to take some action, with or without consultation with local organisations, it is essential that the representatives from leading voluntary bodies should discuss the implementation of practical or financial aid. We must avoid building up yet another official department which would by its very nature absorb the strength that local voluntary bodies need so urgently.

The important thing is that both before and after the announcement of Government plans in the field of youth voluntary service, conferences to discuss the way forward should be held with strong representation from organisers of volunteers already active throughout the country. However much there is to be said for kindling youthful enthusiasm at a national level, there are snags and these must be faced.

A home front movement on the imaginative scale of the American Peace Corps is a most attractive prospect. Government encouragement will do much to blow away the cobwebs in local councils, and national financial support could really put many a local movement on its feet. What then are the possible snags? The first and most important is the danger of undermining local inspiration through a centrally directed plan. It must never be forgotten that ultimate success within any community depends upon the sustained enthusiasm of youngsters on the spot. Any attempt to direct them from above, or from some remote authority, could crush the zeal upon which all depends. It is imperative to avoid the kind of central direction that would stunt imaginative growth and enterprise at local level.

Second, and closely linked with it, is the danger of infringing healthy independence. Young people should be encouraged to respond to the needs round them in ways that they themselves conceive and understand. Guidance from experienced voluntary workers can be most helpful, but must never amount to dictation of method. Patterns of development are bound to vary from place to place and, indeed, should be encouraged to do so.

Third, we must never forget the psychology of approaching youngsters. If in our enthusiastic realisation of the benefits of community service by young people we begin to dragoon them into it wholesale, the cause is as good as lost. Once young people begin to think that community service is something the adult world is telling them to do they will shy from it. Only when it is their own natural response to need and challenge will they become wholeheartedly involved.

I hope that if a national director is appointed, he will be wise enough to bear these points in mind, for his success will largely depend on it. Enough organisational experience has, however, now been accumulated to justify such a hope.

Other snags may occur at the level of the volunteer, for if great numbers are swept into action on initial waves of enthusiasm the likelihood is that the impetus will not last long. It is comparatively easy to arouse emotional zeal among young people, but the problem is to sustain it in practical action over a period of years. This is not simply a matter of organisation. It is also a matter of contact and youth leadership. The rumoured idea of sending out teams of volunteers to villages and towns throughout the country to begin community service schemes is basically good, providing local young people are fully involved in the planning from the outset, on an equal footing, and the right kind of leadership is left behind when the trained teams move on.

It would be wise, also, for any council running such a national programme to have strong provincial representation. Politicians of all parties have been given a salutary reminder in recent by-elections of the strength of regional feelings. Resentment at what is sometimes felt to be remote central dictation on local matters is not confined to Scotland and Wales. We should be very wary of creating it in the sphere of community service.

Yet another danger must be avoided at all costs. This is the impression that the Government will be using young people as a cheap method of supplementing the National Health Service. There is a definite risk of such a belief developing, and not only among cynics. Governments must therefore make it crystal clear that their motives are humanitarian and not political. This is one area in which politics must be kept out. Certainly, it would be most unfortunate if any political party sought to make capital out of what is essentially a non-political, idealistic response of youth to social need. That is why it is so important that supervision and control should be maintained at the local level.

These reservations do not diminish the exciting possibilities that are opened out by Government encouragement and support. Young people need help to overcome the obstacles and inertia that so often face them. When all has been done, however, within the power of a central organisation, the whole movement will live or die by local keenness and inspiration. Instructions on how these can be roused and organised are given in the Appendices.

It must not be forgotten that these are still pioneer days in voluntary service by young people. The situation is changing all the time with remarkable rapidity in the field of service itself, quite apart from the intentions of Government or local organisations. It is changing in the context of the total pattern of community and social development in Britain. Fundamental and revolutionary changes in attitude and structure are undoubtedly imminent. The inadequacy of the present position is widely acknowledged. The momentum is bound to increase so that the ethos in which service is done either by youngsters or adults will certainly be radically different within a decade. Even the term "volunteer service" may be outmoded as the full implications are grasped. No more than in the world of cricket can the artificial distinction between "gentleman" and "players" be long maintained. A professional social worker is no less a volunteer, because he has volunteered his whole life, often for scant reward in material terms.

Similarly, it is now increasingly recognised that those in need are not simply people to whom good must be done. Our aims are both far greater than this and much more revolutionary. What we seek to create is a caring community, wholly integrated and involved at all levels. Our young people are abreast of these developments and face the exciting prospects unfolding before them with an imagination and energy not often achieved by their elders. They are the "Red Guards" of Britain today, or "Blue Guards" if we prefer a colour more symbolic of peaceful intentions. Their aims are just as revolutionary, but their methods and motives are entirely different. They have in common with the young of China a deep rooted desire to create a new future, but they are not regimented or indoctrinated by the State. Where the Chinese Red Guards destroy and abuse, the young volunteers of Britain create compassion and concern. While the majority of Communist youth is deliberately taught to shake angry fists, our young volunteers extend helping hands. There is a world of difference, and in the struggle for human values let us not neglect or under-rate the importance of what our own young people are doing today, very largely on their own initiative.

By their enthusiasm and energy they are already creating a more compassionate and involved community. They are not interested in, and must not be lost in, vertical organisational structures, hide-bound by rule and precept. Such vertical divisions, both in the statutory and volunteer fields of service, are the bane of true social development in Britain. Though many of these organisations are excellent in themselves they have too often become resistant to change, the captives of their own constitutions and hierarchical structure. This must not be allowed to happen to young volunteers.

In our locality we are seeking to change all this by a "Good Neighbour" scheme similar to the excellent "Fish" Good Neighbour scheme carried out in Cambridge by the Council of Churches, and now extending to other parts of the country. Recently we have gained the keen support of local churches for our "Good Neighbour" scheme following their successful "People Next Door" campaign.

The Solihull Council of Social Service has asked the young volunteers to carry out an experimental pilot survey in one district. The aim is to revive community spirit within a whole neighbourhood. Wardens will be asked to adopt a number of homes in their street and to bring neighbourly help to any situation where, through infirmity or emergency, it is needed. Young people will be invited to co-operate with the wardens in bringing necessary aid to people in their district. It is hoped that in this way many youngsters who are unattached to schools or youth groups will become involved, and be the eyes and ears of the young volunteers in their own streets.

Even more important than this, the co-operation which should grow between the generations may well recreate the sense of community which has been so disastrously eroded in twentieth-century Britain.

If it is true that we have been careless in many aspects of our responsibility to society and to young people it is equally true that there is more promise for the future. Alarmists will be able to present a gloomier picture. Increases in juvenile crime, senseless vandalism, teen-age sexual licence and drug addiction are real enough problems. Young people are not all saints or heroes. They are too often the products of our own neglect of spiritual values and of their welfare. "Broken" homes produce "broken" children. Selfish materialism breeds reckless vandalism and contempt in the young.

There is a challenge to us all to become more involved in the social problems of our age. Young and old, Christian and humanist, professional social worker and lay volunteer, all of us are in this together. We dare not neglect the often desperate and ever-increasing needs of the society in which we live. The situation is already more urgent than many realise or care to admit.

And yet, I hope that this book has been able to show a very different and more promising picture of today's youth, full of hope for the future. Youth can, and will, come to the rescue, and in so doing rescue themselves and the nation in the years to come.

Appendices

METHODS AND ORGANISATIONS

IF THROUGH READING this book, you have become aware of the social distress in your own district, and feel prompted to start a similar venture, the following points should prove helpful.

I. How to start a Youth Voluntary Service Group

A. At the outset make sure there are a number of youngsters prepared to support such a scheme. This need only be the members of one youth group or school with which the organiser is associated.

B. Make a survey of the community needs of the area, without arousing undue anticipation.

This should be done through any of the following:
1. The local observation of potential volunteers.
2. The Chief Welfare Officer.
3. The Local Council of Social Service.
4. The Housing Officer.
5. The Children's Welfare Officer.
6. Divisional Welfare Officer of the Red Cross.
7. Local branches of Toc H, Rotary Clubs, Round Tables, Association for the Blind, Societies for Physically or Mentally Handicapped, Women's Royal Voluntary Service, and any other voluntary agency in the district.

8. Doctors and District Nurses.
9. Clergy and Church organisations.
10. Matrons, Wardens, Secretaries and Head teachers of local institutions.

C. When these approaches have given a comprehensive picture of local needs, form a policy planning committee of the young people involved, and decide which areas of service should be tackled. First priority should be given to elderly and handicapped people living on their own.

D. Invite other groups of young people to join as it becomes evident that the needs in the district are too great to be satisfied by your own group unaided. Head teachers and Youth leaders should be approached.

E. Obtain the advice and support of national organisations which have experience in this field. These include: Community Service Volunteers, Christian Education Movement, International Voluntary Service and Toc H. (For addresses see Appendix VI.)

By the time of publication, or shortly thereafter, a national task force may have been formed with Government backing. This will in no way replace the need for local initiative and planning, but should be able to give considerable assistance. It will certainly take many months, or even years, for such nationally organised aid to reach every part of the country, and local enthusiasm should not be frustrated or restrained in the meantime.

F. See that the machinery of administration ensures continuity and reliability, but is at no point overweighted with adults.

II. How to Brief Volunteers

A. HINTS FOR VOLUNTEERS VISITING PRIVATE HOMES

1. Keep all appointments at the time arranged.
2. If a first visit, give your letter of introduction and ask in what ways you can be of service.
3. Stay long enough to make the visit worthwhile and to achieve any specific purpose, but not too long. Remember old people often tire easily.
4. Be cheerful, confident and neat in appearance.
5. Always be polite and show consideration.
6. Take careful note of anything that can be done to help. Do not always wait to be asked, but *make* suggestions.
7. Do any job thoroughly, complete it, and *clear up* afterwards.
8. Try to think out topics of conversation which will be of interest. Remember the person you visit will be interested in you and your affairs, but be a good listener too.
9. If you make a personal promise to do something always do it, but do not make unverified promises on behalf of your group, or of others.
10. Be regular in your service. If for any reason you cannot go:

    i. Tell the person concerned.
    ii. Arrange a substitute if possible.
    iii. Tell your secretary if you cannot do so.
    iv. Do your best to go next time.

11. Arrange outings and entertainments occasionally.
12. If your service fails to satisfy you, you may be sure it is not satisfying the person you serve.

    i. Ask yourself why, and see if you can put it right.
    ii. If this is impossible, see your secretary who will advise you and arrange another job.

B. Hints for the Volunteers visiting Hospitals or Institutions

1. Report to the Matron, Ward Sister or Warden on arrival, and politely ask permission to visit. If it is a first visit present your letter of introduction.
2. Ask if there is any particular service required of you. If not, go into the lounge or ward and introduce yourself confidently and cheerfully. If it is your first visit, Matron or Sister will probably do that for you.
3. Go prepared with one or more of the following:

    i. Bright conversation on topics likely to be of interest.
    ii. Magazines, newspapers or books.
    iii. Projector and films or slides.
    iv. Tape recorder or record player.
    v. Model theatre or puppet show.
    vi. Guitar or other solo instrument and folk songs.
    vii. Art or craftwork.
    viii. Knitting, embroidery or sewing.
    ix. Playing cards or bingo cards.
    x. Pen and notepaper for taking down shopping lists or writing letters.

4. Vary your programme unless your weekly visit is looked forward to for a specific purpose, e.g. shopping, trolley and library book service, or a special arts and crafts evening.
5. Get to know the people in your Home or Ward personally. Though some will be easier than others to get on with, try not to neglect anyone.
6. Arrange your times to fit in with the daily routine.
7. Remember the people you are visiting are in their own home. Even if they are only in hospital for a few days it is home to them at that time. You are their guest just as much as if you were in their private house. Observe the same courtesies.
8. Persuade your parents or other adults to take them out with you occasionally in a car, and with the help of your group organisation arrange periodic outings. It is important to make sure that Matron is agreeable to these trips and that they fit in with her timetable.

The above hints, though by no means exhaustive, should form a useful basis for volunteers undertaking service for the first time. They can be discussed at briefing sessions or given to the volunteers as hand-outs by their group secretaries.

III. Aids to Group Organisation

FROM TIME TO TIME it is necessary to send out correspondence either from the group as a whole, or from one section. It is advisable at an early stage to purchase headed notepaper, as this will save time, look more efficient, and help to gain recognition of the work being done.

Start by introducing a good filing system. This is invaluable, for without one serious blunders are made. The system chosen should not be too complicated or involve a team of volunteers in tedious paper work. Routine work is made easier if proper records are kept. Forms should be filled in by incoming volunteers, showing such important details as where they want to serve and at what times they will be available. It is obviously important to know, too, their preferences in voluntary work and any individual talents or interests they may have. The school or youth group, home address and telephone number of every member should also be recorded.

In addition to any forms, hand-outs and letters used, it is a good policy to have a card index for each group secretary, with a master index of duplicate copies of all the volunteer and service cards held by the General Secretary. It may be felt that a Volunteer Card system is not necessary where application forms have been properly filled in, as it will duplicate some of the information given. There is, however, a great advantage in being able to flick through a card index system to find out at a moment's notice who is available for what. There ought, in any case, to be a good alphabetical record of people and institutions served. The layout of the following three cards may prove helpful:

A. VOLUNTEER CARD

——————— YOUNG VOLUNTEERS

NAME (in full)

ADDRESS

Date of Birth

Tel. No.

School or Youth Group

Date Joined   Date Left

Service Preferences: (i)   (ii)   (iii)

Times and Frequency of Service

Transport: On foot ( )   Bike ( )   Car ( )

Companion in Service

Other Information

Record of Service

B. SERVICE CARD

——————— YOUNG VOLUNTEERS

NAME

Age (Approx.)   Birthday

ADDRESS

Date Service Began

Doctor's Name

Date Service Ended

Tel. No.

Reason

Living Arrangements (with relatives, alone, flat, etc.)

Is Person Served: (i) Active ( )   (ii) Housebound ( )

(iii) Bedridden ( )

Any Physical Disabilities?

How Often do Friends and Relatives Visit?

Type of Service Required

Times and Frequency of Service

Who First asked …Y.V. to Help?

Group/School Volunteers Serving

C. INSTITUTION CARD

——————— YOUNG VOLUNTEERS

NAME OF INSTITUTION

ADDRESS

Tel. No.

Name of Person in Charge

Types of Service Required

Times and Days of Service

Number of Volunteers Needed per Day

School Groups Sending Volunteers

Secretaries Responsible

Names of Serving Volunteers

Other Voluntary Organisations Giving Service

IV. Principles of large Co-operative Schemes

CERTAIN PRINCIPLES are involved in the organisation of a successful voluntary service group. It must not, however, be thought that any one pattern is right in all circumstances.

The two large Midland schemes which have been considered in this book followed quite different patterns of organisation because of their different circumstances, although the "clearing house" principle is common to both.

Some schools are content to develop their own schemes in their own way. One large Coventry comprehensive school began community service through separate House units. Youth clubs often prefer to undertake periodic projects, thereby making allowance for fluctuations in membership. Nevertheless the benefits have been considerable from co-operation between schools and youth clubs of all kinds to the common good.

The main advantages of a co-operative scheme are as follows:

1. The integrating value within a community of young people from all kinds of schools and youth groups working together for the benefit of the rest of that community.

2. The avoidance of unnecessary overlapping of services throughout the area, and undue rivalry in seeking opportunities for service.

3. The value of sharing the experiences of other groups, and the formation of new ideas and plans.

4. The strength of being united when approaching other authorities and organisations.

5. The ability to muster greater numbers of volunteers for any large scale programme or project.

6. It is possible to bring high calibre leadership into the policy planning committees.

Within such a co-operative scheme it is desirable that each group is autonomous in its own development and planning. It should encourage group initiative, but be prepared to co-ordinate activity through a central council.

The young people should play a full part at the policy planning level, both in the establishment of such a scheme and in its maintenance. The role of the adult ought to be inspirational and advisory. Adult executive authority should be used only to ensure harmonious continuity and to overcome any crisis.

If we want voluntary service by the young to be a powerful force in society we must recognise both their right and their ability to play a leading role in its organisation.

V. Organisation of the Solihull Volunteers

A. This depends upon a central council of group Secretaries, which meets several times a term under the leadership of the boy or girl chosen to be General Secretary for the year. The adult President attends only in an advisory capacity.

B. The secretaries are chosen by their groups from the final school year and are helped by assistants who are expected to succeed them when they leave school.

C. The practice is growing of appointing specialist volunteers to take responsibility for particular aspects of service, e.g. decorating, work with the physically handicapped, and entertainments.

D. Group secretaries are responsible for publicity within their schools, recruitment of volunteers, general supervision of service done, and relating the right kind of service to the best volunteer. They are also responsible for any specific projects undertaken by their school in social activities, developing "esprit de corps", or raising funds. They maintain their group records and filing systems and pass duplicate copies to the general secretary for central records.

E. The General Secretary and two assistants see that the machinery of organisation is efficiently maintained. They seek out jobs and projects, and maintain contact with other voluntary and statutory organisations in the social service field. They deal with outside publicity affecting the organisation and hold regular conferences with the adult president. The General Secretary is responsible, also, for seeing that full minutes of all council meetings are recorded, that the filing records are kept up-to-date, and that volunteers are supplied with the necessary forms, information and guidance. For these purposes periodic newsletters are issued. (At times of pre-examination pressure the General Secretary is relieved of exacting responsibilities by someone not involved in examinations. It is noteworthy that secretaries usually obtain good examination results.)

F. The training of volunteers is undertaken at general meetings and conference week-ends held during the year. One of the week-ends is devoted specifically to the training of secretaries. The local Education Authority gives grant-aid towards these courses.

G. Except where fund raising is of a local nature, the group does not become involved in general fund raising activities, and does not take part in flag days, or house-to-house collections, however good their cause.

H. For its own running expenses the group (a) receives grant aid from the local Council of Social Service to meet decorating costs and insurance premiums, (b) organises social activities and dances, (c) receives from sections the proceeds of whist drives, jumble sales or "bring and buy" sales.

I. Whenever possible it is advisable that there should be present a member of staff from each school or youth group to take an advisory interest in the proceedings.

J. Representatives from group councils are delegated to attend meetings of the local Youth Council and the local Council of Social Service so that they are kept in touch with all developments.

K. The group's council discusses and plans policy, and deals with any problems. At meetings enlisting volunteer forms are dealt with, requests for service considered and projects planned. Secretaries delegate among themselves any special responsibilities and arrange social activities. They also arrange to give what assistance they can to the work of the Birmingham Young Volunteers' Trust of which they are a sponsoring authority.

L. Transport is arranged by calling upon school buses, cars of senior volunteers or their parents, the loan of the local Physically Handicapped Society mini-bus, and cars of members of local churches and the local branch of Rotary.

SCHOOLS IN THE SOLIHULL YOUNG VOLUNTEERS SCHEME

Arden High School
Harold Cartwright Grammar School for Girls
Harold Malley Grammar School for Boys
King's High School for Girls, Warwick
Lyndon High School for Girls
Olton Court Convent School
Packwood E. S. N. School for Boys
Saint Martin's School
Sharman's Cross High School for Girls
Solihull High School for Girls (Malvern Hall)
Solihull School
Solihull Technical College
Tudor Grange Grammar School for Girls
Tudor Grange Grammar School for Boys

Numerous youth clubs and fellowships also participate.

VI. Chart Summary of Voluntary Service Opportunities

A. SERVICE TO PEOPLE IN PRIVATE HOMES

Those requiring service	Kinds of service possible	Persons to contact
Elderly and Physically Handicapped People	Visiting—Shopping —Gardening—Decorating—Housework —Reading—Entertaining—Sharing Hobbies—Walks— Outings—Wheelchair service—Preparing Meals— Repairs	Welfare Officer Housing Officer District Nurses Doctors. Clergy Relatives Red Cross. W.R.V.S.
Blind, Deaf and Dumb People	Visiting—Housework —Shopping—Outings—Walks— Sharing Hobbies— Preparing Meals— Home Repairs. For the Blind—Tape Recordings, Records. For the Deaf—Slides, Films.	Local Association for Blind, Deaf or Dumb Welfare Officer Relatives Red Cross Toc H
Mentally Handicapped Children and their Parents	Outings—Walks— Entertainment—Repairing Toys—Art— Music—Sitting-in for Parents—Outdoor Activities and Amusements	Local Society for Mentally Handicapped Relatives

Those requiring service	*Kinds of service possible*	*Persons to contact*
Deprived Families and Children	Running Play-groups —Manning Adventure Playgrounds— Helping with Camps and Holidays— Taking Children into Parks—Distributing Fuel, Gifts, Clothing, at Christmas and other times —Visiting—Decorating—Repairs	Welfare Officer Children's Officer Family Service Unit Council of Social Service

B. Service in Institutions

General Hospitals and Nursing Homes	Reception Service— Preparing Dressings —Visiting Wards, especially Geriatric Wards—Serving Meals—Trolley Service—Changing Beds —Reading—Entertaining—Helping to Walk Patients in Hospital Grounds	Matron Hospital Secretary Chairman of Friends of the Hospital
Mental Hospitals and Homes	Visiting—Taking Patients for Walks— Running Art & Craft Groups— Hobbies—Entertainments—Serving Meals—Outings to Pantomimes and Zoos—Help in Workshops—Support on Open Days	Doctor or Psychiatrist. Chief Male Nurse. Matron
Schools for the Educationally Sub-Normal	Arranging Games and Hobbies— Outdoor Activities and Team Competitions—Camps—Folksinging	Head Teacher Matron

Those requiring service	*Kinds of service possible*	*Persons to contact*
Schools for the Physically Handicapped and Blind, Children's Homes and Reception Centres	Serving Meals—Help in Dormitories—Bathing Children—Classroom Assistance with Modelling, Reading, Art—Outdoor Activities and Team Games—Swimming Instruction—Take Home to Tea—Outings and Walks	Head Teacher Matron Warden
Old People's Homes	Visiting—Shopping—Library Service—Reading—Tape Recording—Serving Meals—Outings—Wheelchair Service—Letter Writing—Hobbies—Arts and Crafts	Matron or Warden Secretary of Home or Welfare Officer Residents Near Relatives

C. SERVICE TO SOCIETY

Local Community	Improvement of Derelict Sites—Removal of Disused Huts—Abandoned Cars—Litter	Local Authority Civic Trust Community Assoc.
General Public	Reclamation of Public Footpaths and Waterways—Slag Heaps—Repairs to Fences and Signposts	Local Authority Civic Trust
Homes and Institutions	Restoration of Grounds, Hedge Trimming—Path Laying—Lawn Care	Hospital Matron or Secretary Wardens

VII. Addresses of Voluntary Service Organisations

THE FOLLOWING list gives some of the major organisations at present known to be active in this field, but the situation is changing so rapidly that many new groups are springing up in different parts of the country. It is bound to be incomplete.

A. LOCAL YOUTH VOLUNTARY SERVICE GROUPS

Birmingham Young Volunteers' Trust
25 Spring Road, Birmingham 15
(CAL. 1175)   Organising Officer: Miss Jane Markham

Bristol "Service 9"
9 Elmdale Road, Bristol 8.
(Bristol 25998)   Organising Officer: Mr. Peter Gilliat

Community Council of Lancashire
Selmec House, Wynnstay Grove, Manchester
(RUS. 3366)   General Secretary: Mr. J. S. Jackson

Enterprise Youth
8 Palmerston Place, Edinburgh 12
(CAL. 5890)   Secretary: Mr. J. B. Frizell

Manchester Youth & Community Service
Langton House, 82 Gt. Bridgewater St.
Manchester 1
(236 6754)   Chairman: Mr. B. G. Phythian

"Operation X" Coventry
8 Priory Road, Coventry
(Coventry 29242)

Sevenoaks Volunteer Service Unit
(Apply Sevenoaks School for information)

Shrewsbury Schools Committee
4 Dogpole, Shrewsbury
(53090)
Organising Secretary Shropshire Council of Social Service:
Mr. R. A. Nunn

Solihull Young Volunteers
President: Mr. L. C. Bailey, Solihull School, Warwickshire
(SOL. 2629 or SOL. 4409)

1964—Task Force
3–7 Old Queen Street, London S.W.1
(WHI. 3765)   Founder-Organiser: Mr. A. Steen

Voluntary Community Service
2, Cathedral Road, Cardiff 27625

Young Volunteers of Merseyside
14 Castle Street, Liverpool 2
(CEN. 7728)   Development Officer: Mr. G. R. Eustance

Youth Action Sheffield
Social Service House
69 Division Street, Sheffield 1
(Sheffield 24041 Ext. 8)   Organiser: Mr. Peter Furniss

Youth Enterprise in the North-East
c/o Civic Trust for the North-East
26, Sutton Street, Durham 61182

Youth Action York
c/o York Community Council
10, Priory Street, York 54524

B. NATIONAL YOUTH VOLUNTARY SERVICE ORGANISATIONS

Christian Education Movement
Annandale, North End Road, London N.W.11
(MEA 4366)
Secretary Schools Committee: Miss Sheila M. Hobden

Community Service Volunteers
Toynbee Hall, 28 Commercial Street, London E.1
(BIS 8113)   Founder and Hon. Director: Mr. Alec Dickson

Council for Nature Conservation Corps
Zoological Gardens, Regents Park, N.W.1
(722 7111)
(Specialising in week-end clearance work, replanting, etc.)

National Council of Social Service
26 Bedford Square, London, W.C.1
(MUS 4066)
(Apply to Youth Department)

Volunteer Emergency Service
1 Plough Lane, Wallington, Surrey
(WAL 6183)   Founder-Organiser: Mrs. M. Ryerson
(Motorists and motor-cyclists rush drugs, blood and specimens to
    hospitals and laboratories)

"Toc H" Mobile Action
15 Trinity Square, London E.C.3

C. YOUTH VOLUNTARY SERVICE ORGANISATIONS
      SPECIALISING IN OVERSEAS SERVICE

British Council of Churches
10 Eaton Gate, Sloane Square
London S.W.1
(SLO 9611)   Youth Department Secretary: Rev. Thorley Roe

British Volunteer Programme
26 Bedford Square, London W.C.1
(MUS 4066)   Secretary: Mr. Philip Zealey

Catholic Institute for International Relations
38 King Street, London W.C.2
(TEM 1973)   Organiser: Mr. S. Windass

International Voluntary Service
72 Oakley Square, London N.W.1
(EUS 3195)

United Nations Association International Service
93 Albert Embankment, London S.E.1
(REL 0181)   Deputy General Secretary: Mr. D. E. Chance

Voluntary Service Overseas
3 Hanover Street, London W.1
(HYD 0501)

Quaker Work Camps
Friends House, Euston Road, London N.W.1
(EUS 3601)   Secretary: Mrs. Erika Carter